ELLE DECOR

THE HEIGHT
of STYLE

ELLE DECOR

THE HEIGHT of STYLE

INSPIRING IDEAS
FROM THE WORLD'S CHICEST ROOMS

Michael Boodro and the Editors of ELLE DECOR
Text by Ingrid Abramovitch

ABRAMS, NEW YORK

Editor: Rebecca Kaplan
Creative Director: Florentino Pamintuan
Designer: Alexander Wolf
Production Manager: Erin Vandeveer

Library of Congress Control Number: 2014930554

ISBN: 978-1-4197-0992-0

Printed and bound in China

10 9 8 7 6 5 4 3 2 1

Abrams books are available at special discounts when purchased in quantity
for premiums and promotions as well as fundraising or educational use.
Special editions can also be created to specification. For details, contact
specialsales@abramsbooks.com or the address below.

115 West 18th Street
New York, NY 10011
www.abramsbooks.com

CONTENTS

INTRODUCTION   7

CLASSICAL   8

FANCIFUL   70

PRACTICAL   114

PERSONAL   174

ELLE DECOR'S SOURCEBOOK   220

PHOTO CREDITS   222

ACKNOWLEDGMENTS   224

INTRODUCTION

One of the great pleasures of editing ELLE DECOR is being able to see the wildly different ways that people choose to live. We have always published homes in a broad range of styles—we're not limited to a single aesthetic, or dogmatic in our idea of what constitutes beauty. The magazine has never equated quality with money, or personal style with trendiness. Throughout ELLE DECOR's 25 years, I have been a fan of its stylistic diversity, the wide range of designers it covers, the talented photographers it employs, its global perspective, and its appreciation of fashion, flair, and fun.

This book is, in some ways, a compilation of the best rooms we have published in the past five years. But how do you define the best? We didn't want simply to compile a volume of our "greatest hits." We wanted to do a bit more, to provide a way to think about the rooms we chose, why they work, and what makes them so appealing.

Whatever its style—restrained and monochromatic, vivid and exuberant, or eclectic and surprising—a successful interior is cohesive. It demands discipline, editing, and a clear and consistent point of view. A home is no more a conglomeration of disparate rooms than a novel is a compendium of random words. There is always an overarching vision. Looking over the hundreds of homes we have published since 2009, I realized that they could be organized into four categories, and that is how we have structured this book, into chapters titled Classical, Fanciful, Practical and Personal.

These are broad terms, and some of the rooms in one chapter could easily fit in another (all rooms are practical, after all, in that they serve a purpose—even if it's only to show off). But I believe that the categories can be useful in thinking about design. And we have supplemented the photographs with insights from professionals, and pointers and principles on what makes certain rooms so successful.

So no matter the style of your own house or apartment, or in what category you might place it, we hope that you will find something useful and pertinent within these pages, something that will not only dazzle your eye but also help you achieve a home that is the height of style.

Michael Boodro
Editor in Chief, ELLE DECOR

CLASSICAL

Some rooms are unabashedly iconoclastic—this is decor that exclaims: Look at me! But when most of us come home, a strong statement is not what we're looking for. Quite the opposite: We want personal environments imbued with a sense of order and calm. In the decorating world, classical rooms have always been among the most popular. In these soothing spaces, nothing is jarring. Balance and proportion rule.

The ancient Greeks and Romans were the first to form the classical language of design with its emphasis on geometry and regularity of scale. They took inspiration for their temples and villas from nature's own artistry—from the mirror-image marvel of a butterfly's iridescent wings to the symmetry of the human form. "Proportion," wrote the Roman architect and author Vitruvius, "is that agreeable harmony between the several parts of a building." In the world of interior design, it's a credo that still resonates.

The beauty of a classical scheme is that it is innately flexible. This isn't about incorporating antique columns and busts into a room (though in the right hands—Axel Vervoordt's or David Easton's, for instance—those elements can indeed be sublime). It's also not confined to any one style: Both traditional and modern spaces can take a classical approach. Rather, the goal is to design rooms where everything is in balance—to achieve, decorwise, an overall state of grace and an atmosphere of serenity. A classical room does the thinking for you. In terms of layout, there is a logic that feels inevitable (but was clearly labored over). Often, the space is oriented around a focal point, whether it is a fireplace, a dining table, a console in an entry, or the headboard in the bedroom. However the designer or homeowner got there, one can't imagine the room any other way. Classical decor can still hold surprises: On pages 32–33, the interior designer Steven Gambrel counterintuitively transforms a reception hall into a dining room, with a staircase as the backdrop for a rectangular dining table framed by matching Louis XIV chairs.

In some of the classical rooms in this chapter, monochromatic schemes—sometimes neutral, sometimes in hues inspired by nature—are enlivened by subtle touches of bolder color. For decorator Celerie Kemble, tranquility is a blue-gray bedroom offset with warm touches of gold, as seen on page 49. Despite its apparent simplicity, creating a classic room is not easy. There is no formula. It takes a rigorous eye to pull it off. One needs to understand the hierarchies of space as well as have an appreciation for scale and proportion. Furniture and objects must be edited down to the essentials. The more minimal the look, the more unforgiving it can be, which is why good-quality finishes and fine architectural details can make or break these spaces. These are rooms that whisper, rather than shout, with special details that can take time to reveal themselves: a subtle mix of textures, or unique finishing touches such as custom hardware or passementerie.

And because even a harmonious life isn't always perfect, the art of decorating a classical room often lies in knowing when to color outside of the lines. Not everything has to be in pairs. Sometimes, it's that one-off chair that breaks the symmetry of a room, or an animating burst of sparkle, that can bring an entire space to life.

"THE APARTMENT FEELS MUCH LARGER NOW BECAUSE ROOMS HAVE CERTAIN PURPOSES, SPACES ARE DEFINED, AND VIEWS ARE FRAMED. THERE IS A LOGICAL SEQUENCE TO IT"

William Sofield, interior designer

LEFT: In the living room of an apartment designed by William Sofield for a Manhattan couple, the soigné decor feels glamorous yet relaxed owing to a traditional floor plan where numerous elements—from chairs to mirrors and lamps—are employed in pairs. Soothing textures and gleaming accents amplify the purity and elegance of the room.

FACING PAGE: To make the long, two-story living room at her Ojai ranch feel more intimate, Reese Witherspoon, working with designer Kristen Buckingham, divided the space into two distinct areas: a small sitting area by the massive fireplace and a more casual area (not shown) with a games table and bar. The furnishings, from European antiques to rustic pieces, echo the brick and stucco architecture of the historic Wallace Neff house.

LEFT: In filmmaker Michael Bay's Miami home, which was decorated by Lynda Murray, a glass-and-steel staircase designed by architect Chad Oppenheim rises three stories to the roof deck. The sinuous stair is reflected in the living area's white limestone floor.

BELOW: In a London duplex designed by Paolo Moschino for Sofia and Niccolo Barattieri di San Pietro, a pair of matching tables in the dining area give a sense of symmetry to the space while adding flexibility. When separated, the tables allow for intimate groupings; pushed together, they form a long surface that can accommodate large gatherings.

FACING PAGE: The dining area of decorator Steven Volpe's San Francisco loft features a George Nakashima–inspired table in live-edge walnut. The table's square shape is designed so that twelve can sit around it and converse over dinner.

ELLE DECOR contributing design editor Cynthia Frank created a loggia for her Southampton, New York, home that was inspired by classical French interiors. The space has French doors, blue-and-white furnishings, and a diamond-patterned marble floor.

"ATMOSPHERE IS THE
MOST ESSENTIAL ELEMENT
IN A ROOM. IT'S THE
ONE THING YOU CAN'T BUY. IT'S
NOT ABOUT AN
OBJECT; IT'S ABOUT THE
END RESULT"

Charlotte Moss,
decorator

LEFT: In an 18th-century Paris apartment designed by François-Joseph Graf for the English antiques dealer Piers von Westenholz, the library is encased in custom bookshelves with classical detailing. An 18th-century English desk and early 1700s Italian mirror add to the room's timeless style.

ABOVE: In her Aspen, Colorado, getaway, Charlotte Moss balances the heft of a Louis XIII mantel worthy of a French château with a stacked-stone fireplace that is more characteristic of the homes in the area.

Interior designer Peter Mikic hired craftsmen in India to carve Adam-style marble fireplace surrounds for his London townhouse, such as the one in this drawing room. The traditional architecture sets off the room's more contemporary elements, including artwork by David Hockney and an over-scale curved velvet sofa.

WHAT THE PROS KNOW: *FINESSE*

PARE IT DOWN

Use architectural details to create a sense of structure and symmetry. Features like wall paneling, pilasters in doorways, French doors, and patterned floors can enhance a room's classical feeling. In the library of the Paris apartment on pages 18–19, interior designer François-Joseph Graf houses the homeowner's extensive book collection in built-in bookshelves with moldings resembling classical columns.

SMALL REFINEMENTS

The more minimal the look, the more that such elements as high-quality finishes, well-crafted upholstery, and fine architectural details count. In Courteney Cox's living room on page 67, bronzed-steel trim on windows, oak floors, and a flagstone fire-place make the contemporary room feel unique and handmade.

FINE LINES

Use a variety of textures to create depth and personality in a room, from fabrics to wall surfaces to floors. Silks and velvets add glamour, reclaimed wood brings patina and age, and mirrors and metallics give a room shimmer and sparkle. In Jean-Louis Deniot's Paris living room on pages 34–35, a mantel in striped Turkish marble adds a graphic punch to a room with modern lines.

ECLECTIC TOUCH

Even if you adore 18th-century style or Art Deco, it's best not to be overly slavish to any one period: The room will look fresher if you mix in elements from other periods.

Contemporary art will pop against a backdrop of antiques. And not everything has to match. In her Aspen home on page 19, for example, Charlotte Moss balances floral chintz curtains with brawnier elements like tapestry chairs and elk horns.

LIGHT TOUCH

Good lighting is key to an elegant space. Architectural lighting should be unobtrusive: For spotlights, use trimless fixtures to minimize their presence, or conceal lights behind glass panels. Then layer in a mixture of decorative and task lighting. For instance, in the living room on pages 50–51, decorator Alessandra Branca combines a ceiling-hung pendant lamp for ambiance with a floor lamp and wall-hung swing-arm sconces for more direct lighting.

The background of a Manhattan family loft designed by architect Lee Mindel for Winsome Brown and Claude Arpels is largely in whites and neutrals, allowing furniture and objects in primary hues—from a pair of cobalt midcentury chairs to felt Paola Lenti ottomans in yellow and orange—to pop.

ABOVE: In a New York apartment belonging to Theory's Andrew Rosen and Jenny Dyer, which she designed, a palette of cool neutrals lends a feeling of calm to a master bedroom with a suede wall and a sculptural chair by Vladimir Kagan.

RIGHT: A New York family room designed by David Kleinberg contains a traditional seating arrangement with facing white sofas and a quartet of 1930s-style armchairs. An inlaid Indian table and an overscale suede ottoman complete the intimate group.

FACING PAGE: Architect Peter Pennoyer gave a Manhattan living room neoclassical paneling and dentil and crown moldings, creating an elegant backdrop for decorator Victoria Hagan's cream-and-black decor. A contemporary work by Kiki Smith hangs over an antique English mantel.

In Giulia Azmoudeh's London drawing room, which was designed by Paolo Moschino, a dramatic set of prints depicting vipers looks powerful but controlled in a symmetrical wall display that fits perfectly within the wall's paneling.

ANATOMY OF A ROOM

In a château in the Normandy region of France, the salon's 18th-century architecture provides a classical framework that allows the home-owner—Gérard Tremolet, whose firm creates embroideries for couturiers and interior designers—the freedom to experiment with bold color and decorative embellishments.

- **TAKE LIBERTIES** Even in an antique home, don't be slavish to period. Tremolet's goal was to create a fresh, playful version of grand 18th-century style. "If you're looking for historical accuracy, there are huge mistakes," he admits. "I simply drew on my imagination, as well as from films like *Barry Lyndon*."

- **A TOUCH OF WHIMSY** Inspired by such fanciful period murals as those at Versailles, Tremolet hand-painted the walls of his salon with cheeky decorative monkeys dressed in costumes. Meanwhile, the chandelier's candlesticks are topped with shades in a fashionable leopard pattern.

- **JEWEL TONES** The room's classical elements and layout ground the space and provide a point of departure for Tremolet's bold and surprising color palette of reds, burgundies, greens, and yellows. Meanwhile, an adjacent hallway echoes the salon's color scheme with its rich red walls and green stools.

- **TACTILE ELEMENTS** The salon's decor contains a harmonious balance of textures. Velvet upholstery and a wool Oriental rug create a cozy atmosphere, while an exuberant crystal chandelier and pair of candelabras add sparkle and glamour to the space.

- **COUTURE TOUCHES** Tremolet, who worked for many years at the heart of the Paris fashion world, gives antique furnishings a makeover with beautifully tailored upholstery. The sofa becomes a showstopper with its red striped velvet cushions and white frame.

- **CUSTOM CARPENTRY** Architectural detail, too, makes the space. The wall panels are framed in gold while the doorway is tall and wide, with a pair of paneled and painted doors.

"WE WEREN'T SLAVES TO HISTORY BUT
WE WERE CERTAINLY INSPIRED BY IT. WE TOOK
THE PIECES THAT WORKED FOR US
AND WERE REALLY KIND TO THE HOUSE"

Steven Gambrel, decorator

ABOVE: On their horse farm in
Kentucky, fashion designers Mark
Badgley and James Mischka used
restraint in furnishing a guest room.
The pared-down furnishings include
vintage equestrian prints and an
antique bed topped with a Ralph
Lauren Home blanket.

RIGHT: Steven Gambrel turned
the reception hall of a Tudor-style
home in Westchester, New York,
into a handsome dining room.
A 1930s English fruitwood table
has rounded edges that echo
the unusual shape of the stair rail,
which is original to the house.

In the living room of his Paris apartment, decorator Jean-Louis Deniot juxtaposes graphic elements—a striped Turkish marble mantel, a bold carpet—that are equally strong and therefore in balance. The room's walls and ceiling feature a mural evocative of the sky by the artist Mathias Kiss. A pair of 1960s Knoll sofas, along with a Directoire chair, frame a cocktail table by Ado Chale.

FACING PAGE: A mahogany table by Rose Tarlow Melrose House anchors the library in agent Lynn Nesbit's Manhattan apartment, which was designed by Bill Brockschmidt and Courtney Coleman. The room incorporates such classical design elements as built-in bookshelves, a library ladder, and English Regency chairs.

BELOW: A palette of pale neutrals creates a harmonious backdrop for a mix of antiques and contemporary furniture and art in interior designer Darryl Carter's townhouse in Washington, D.C. The pair of low cocktail tables are rectangular slabs of poured polished concrete.

RIGHT: The living room of a classic Maynard Woodard midcentury house belonging to Lynn Harris and Matti Leshem in Los Angeles gets a contemporary refresh thanks to decorator Sarah Walker, with new concrete floors and a mix of contemporary furniture and such 20th-century design classics as a Hans J. Wegner chair. The original ceiling of Douglas fir was stripped of years of accumulated paint.

In Ireland's 18th-century Russborough House, the dramatic library retains such original features as a marble fireplace and a plaster ceiling by Paolo and Filippo Lafranchini. The room's furnishings include a 20th-century sofa and armchairs in oxblood leather, a George III–style table in inlaid mahogany, and a portrait of the Countess of Airlie by Sir John Lavery.

WHAT
THE PROS
KNOW:
FLOOR PLANS

LINE IT UP

A clear and symmetrical layout contributes to a sense of harmony in a space and puts people at ease. One way to do this is to create a straightforward floor plan based on a grid—the classic example is a pair of chairs facing a sofa with a cocktail table in the center. In Reese Witherspoon's living room on page 12, a square furniture arrangement in the center of the room balances the extreme height of the space, which seems even taller with its elongated chimney flue.

FOCAL POINTS

Some rooms have a dominant architectural feature that draws the eye—a fireplace mantel, a picture window overlooking the ocean, or a graceful staircase in an entry hall all serve as a natural focus. When none exists, create a point of interest with a prominent piece of furniture, a spectacular painting, or a wall in a contrasting color. A very large room should have more than one focal point. In the expansive living room on pages 10–11, the interior designer Robert Couturier creates several seating groups to anchor the sizable space.

PLAY DOUBLES

In a classical room, think in twos, or multiples of two. Place pairs of objects and furniture in the same position on a vertical axis: matching side tables at opposite ends of a sofa, for instance, or a pair of stools at the foot of a bed. Or create a wall tableau by hanging a set of artworks in identical frames in a square or rectangular grid, as Paolo Moschino does with his framed art series in the London drawing room on pages 28–29.

SHAKE IT UP

Once you have created that symmetry, don't be afraid to break it. Try adding a single unique element—such as a beautiful one-off chair or an interesting side table—to an otherwise balanced floor plan. Or liven things up by adding an unexpected element such as the pair of yellow poufs that William Sofield inserted into the elegant silver-and-gray living room on page 13.

BIG AND SMALL

Consider scale and proportion in the design of a room. In a grand room, go overscale. In a petite space, choose more delicate furnishings. Occasionally a single large piece feels right even in a small room. Take advantage of a room's height: In Julia Reed's New Orleans home on pages 62–63, an elongated mantel mirror and yellow draperies emphasize the height of the walls.

FACING PAGE: The great room of a Mediterranean-style home in Dana Point, California, has a beamed ceiling and Marmorino plaster walls. The space, which was designed by architect Bob White of ForestStudio and M. Elle Design, is decorated in a serene palette of blues, greens, grays, and creams.

ABOVE: Designed by Steven Harris and Lucien Rees Roberts, the Brooklyn brownstone of Remodelista's Francesca Connolly has a dining room with a vintage chandelier and a table made of vintage Knoll bases with an oak top. The dining chairs are equally divided between Saarinen and Eames classics.

Decorator Robert Stilin's minimalist decor for the master bedroom of a 19th-century farmhouse in the Hamptons features a custom-made metal bed, a table that came from a mill, and a Belgian leather chair. The clients, Stilin says, "were insistent that you could keep what's essentially charming about a place and yet make it effortlessly livable for a family."

LEFT: Steven Gambrel's design for the living room of a Manhattan pied-à-terre in the Plaza Hotel features such old-world details as wood wall panels, outlined in black, that were painted with multiple layers of glaze. The room's luxe details include silk velvet and linen upholstery and wool-silk patterned carpeting.

ABOVE: In decorator Michael Smith's New York penthouse, the living room's neoclassical elements include a 19th-century Recamier and a model of a triumphal arch. A photograph by Lynn Davis hangs in front of the custom bookcases, while a matchstick blind allows glimpses of the city beyond.

When decorator Suzanne Rhein
that her Manhattan living room's win
and alcoves would make it difficu
she hired Bob Christian, an artist ar
painter, to create a mural that s
room. The fanciful backdrop sets
18th- and 19th-century antique
Louis XVI chaise and a pair of Italian

ARTEMPO

PALLADIAN STYLE STEVEN PARISSIEN

LEFT: A dining room/library in Manhattan designed by Alex Papachristidis for Michael Field and Jeff Arnstein is an object lesson in symmetry, from the white bookcases that flank the mantel to the matching tufted sofas. Midcentury Danish rosewood chairs surround the dining table by Paul McCobb.

ABOVE: Celerie Kemble's design for a master bedroom for a Manhattan couple, Jane and Michael DeFlorio, has a gray-and-white scheme modeled on fashion designer Christian Dior's iconic Parisian salon. The walls are sheathed in suede with coordinating silk de Gournay draperies.

In decorator Alessandra Branca's Manhattan living room, the walls, carpet, curtain fabric, and sofa upholstery are all in neutral tones, and the room's furnishings include both antiques and functional pieces like a sleeper sofa. "I like the practical next to the elegant and the charge of red and black against the beige," she says. "Black gives rooms depth, and a shot of red is the kick you need in life."

FACING PAGE: The upstate New York country home of architect Steven Harris and interior designer Lucien Rees Roberts features an indoor/ outdoor dining room with sliding glass doors that open onto the garden. The 1960s caster chairs are by Pierre Paulin and the Florence Knoll table base is fitted with a custom Indian laurel-wood top.

ABOVE: In a 1740 house in rural Connecticut owned by Istvan Francer and John Cummins, the living room is furnished with a white Antonio Citterio sofa and Harvey Probber armchairs. Eclectic touches—African cushions, a portrait of a lady, conical glass lamps— add character to the space without distracting from its serenity.

LEFT: A Manhattan living room designed by Bruce T. Bananto for Monica Mandelli and Marco Valla is a study in warm colors played against cool, with minimalist white furniture and a glowing series of golden artworks by Julian Stanczak.

ABOVE: The library of a downtown Manhattan loft designed by Nina Seirafi for Walter Schupfer and Gina Goldman features floor-to-ceiling rosewood bookshelves, a zebra-pattern rug, a velvet sofa, and a brass side table.

RIGHT: The dramatic drawing room of Château de Fleury, a 16th-century French castle owned by Charles de Ganay, has multiple fireplaces, perfectly aged leather armchairs, and generous sofas. The room's furnishings include Baroque chandeliers, a Regency desk and bookshelves, a Louis XV sofa and a red Louis XVI bergère. The room "faces east and benefits from the most lovely light," says de Ganay, who has lived there for over half a century.

WHAT THE PROS KNOW: *COLOR*

OUTSIDE IN

A harmonious color scheme connects to its environment. Look outside for inspiration—a room's palette can be inspired by your garden, the sky, or the architecture of your house. In Cynthia Frank's Southampton loggia on pages 16–17, the blue-and-white upholstery echoes the hues of the sky and pool in the adjacent garden, while potted plants inside provide a visual link to the outdoors. Don't compete with a fabulous view. On pages 58–59, Ralph Lauren's Manhattan apartment, which overlooks Central Park, has a minimalist black-and-white palette that does not detract from the stunning sight lines.

SERENE HUES

Consider adjacent spaces before committing to a room's palette. The colors should flow from room to room. One way to achieve this is to use hues of similar intensities. For example, if you have a gray-green in one room, don't put bright green in the room next to it. Subdued colors help lend a space a relaxed feeling. Decorator Suzanne Rheinstein created a soothing effect in her New York apartment on pages 46–47 with a scheme consisting of grays, creams, taupes, and soft green-blues.

COLOR STATEMENT

To give a room unity, Miles Redd will often bathe it in a single fabulous color. For the living room on pages 64–65, he covered the walls in scarlet felt and upholstered the furniture to match. Try a powerful color as a grand gesture in an otherwise neutral space. In the tailored living room on this page, interior designer Steven Volpe adds drama with draperies in a lush yellow.

OPPOSITES ATTRACT

Complementary colors—shades that are opposites on a color wheel—create a contrast that is perfectly in balance. Lee Mindel succeeds in using strong shades such as cobalt and orange in the room on pages 24–25 because the hues look proportionate.

LEFT: The vibrant yellow silk draperies in this London drawing room are an audacious choice, but it works because of their tailoring. Every piece in the room, which was designed by Steven Volpe for Bita Daryabari, is considered, from the Pierre Paulin daybed to the vintage pendant light by Stilnovo. Picasso's *Personnage en buste* hangs over the sofa.

FACING PAGE: In an 18th-century manor house in Bordeaux, owners Michael Coorengel and Jean-Pierre Calvagrac re-created Louis XVI-style decor in the salon. The room contains a Georges Jacob settee and armchairs, an 18th-century Aubusson rug and chest of drawers, and a chandelier and sconces from the 19th century.

Ralph and Ricky Lauren's minimalist New York duplex, which overlooks Central Park, has a raised living room with dark-wood floors and a custom-made sectional sofa. The room's black-and-white palette is deliberately spare so as not to detract from the view. "It's about the windows, and the light that comes in from the park," he says.

TOP: Decorator Alidad's London yellow drawing room has white wall moldings inset with tiny mirrors. Above the marble mantel, a circa 1930s French gilded mirror is flanked by a pair of 1950s pineapple sconces.

RIGHT: In Michael Coorengel and Jean-Pierre Calvagrac's 18th-century French château, a wall of built-in bookcases is topped with antique busts. The room has a Directoire sofa and an 18th-century armchair with its original needlepoint upholstery.

FACING PAGE: A pair of black-and-white obelisks sets a classical tone in the entry hall of Coorengel and Calvagrac's manor house in Bordeaux. The ceiling was hand-painted and the diamond-patterned marble flooring was laid in a traditional 18th-century design.

Writer Julia Reed's parlor in New Orleans' Garden District has a layout centered on the black Italian marble fireplace, which is original to the house. The faux-bamboo benches are English Regency, while the side table belonged to Reed's great-grandmother.

"WE WANTED TO KEEP IT YOUNG
AND FRESH AND HAPPY.
THE ARCHITECTURE HAS SERIOUSNESS
AND SCHOLARSHIP, BUT THE
PALETTE AND FURNISHINGS ARE
INTENSE AND VIBRANT"

Miles Redd,
interior designer

ABOVE: The black-and-white pattern of a toile de Jouy fabric creates unity when it is applied on the walls, curtains, and bedcover of Daniel Beauchemin and Marc de Laat's bedroom in the Netherlands.

RIGHT: Even a statement-making color like red can fit into a classical scheme, especially when used on both the walls and the furniture, as it is in this Manhattan living room decorated by Miles Redd and renovated by Dick Bories and James Shearron.

ABOVE: Actress Courteney Cox's Malibu living room, designed by Trip Haenisch, has a large white sectional sofa that visually balances the space, with its double-height stone fireplace. The room's furnishings include an oversized vintage French lamp and a Hans Wegner chair.

LEFT: In the Ketchum, Idaho, home of decorator Mary Lynn Turner of M. Elle Designs, a barn was transformed into a dramatic 1,000-square-foot great room clad in reclaimed wood. The dining area is lined in steel bookcases, while a wood-and-iron chandelier is suspended over the oak table.

FACING PAGE: In the library of a Manhattan loft designed by architect Len Morgan, the bookshelves are custom-made and the 1927 light fixture was designed by Erik Gunnar Asplund for his modernist masterpiece, the Stockholm Public Library. The rosewood table is circa-1830 English, the chairs are by Jacques Adnet, and the carpet is Art Deco.

ANATOMY OF A ROOM

In his drawing room in London, interior designer Alidad uses classical proportions and symmetry to create a serene environment that is ideally suited for reading or conversation. The decor is eclectic enough to be interesting, yet carefully balanced so that nothing feels out of place.

- **TALL TALES** In a room with tall ceilings, remember to take advantage of the height of the space. The 17th-century Flemish tapestry fills the wall behind the sofa from floor to ceiling. "I like overscaled things," says Alidad, "and I think that in this room, the tapestry makes the space. I deliberately looked for the biggest tapestry that could fit."

- **CLASSICAL FRAMEWORK** The room's traditional details—from the intricate plaster cornice to the vertical molding strips and paneled door—create a geometry for the space that feels logical and proportionate.

- **FINE TOUCHES** The smallest details can add texture and interest. While most of the room is painted, the corners are covered in a matching raised paper that has a slightly different texture. Meanwhile, Alidad inserted tiny mirrors into the room's white molding strips. "As you move around the room, the mirrors flicker," he says. "Different areas of the room light up."

- **BY CONTRAST** By covering the largest piece of furniture, the sofa, in a quiet white linen, Alidad grounds the space and frees himself to use a variety of patterns and textures throughout.

- **TWO BY TWO** The designer creates the illusion of classical pairings even when the specifics are different. The chairs on either side of the cocktail table may be different in shape and pattern, but their muted blue-and-cream palette gives a sense of balance.

- **WARM IT UP** The soft yellow palette gives unity and warmth to the space and is an ideal choice for a day room. "I always have a yellow room," Alidad says. "It's cheerful."

FANCIFUL

The most memorable rooms are rarely beige. On the contrary, spaces that leave a lasting impression are often over the top. A fanciful room is designed to dazzle. Who could ever forget the sultan's Fruit Room in the harem at the Topkapı Palace, painted floor to ceiling with fruit and flowers? Or the legendary Hall of Mirrors, a long colonnade sparkling with chandeliers and mirrored arches overlooking the gardens at Versailles? There is an inherent theatricality that lies behind these fantastical spaces. No surprise, then, that some of the masters of the genre—from Renzo Mongiardino to Tony Duquette—not only decorated real homes but also designed sets for theater and film.

No question: You have to be brave to create a room that is a jaw-dropper. The designers and homeowners whose showstopping spaces are featured in this chapter most certainly have courage. It takes guts to swathe a room in a single patterned fabric, or lacquer it in a bold color. Audacity is a prerequisite when one commissions handmade boiseries in Paris and then decides to paint them bright orange, as the decorator Robert Couturier did for a client in New York (see pages 90–91). As for Muriel Brandolini, a decorator who never lacks for chutzpah, why not cover a kitchen in rich blue felt that has been hand-beaded and embroidered with the lyrics of the Lou Reed song "Perfect Day," as she did in the project featured on page 93?

With a no-holds-barred room, it's all or nothing—you cannot start the dive and stop in midair. Or as the late Morris Lapidus, the midcentury architect of Miami's neo-Baroque Fontainebleau Hotel, liked to say: "Too much is never enough." The next logical addition, once you have piled on the suzani and the ikat textiles? Anything leopard. Or to take a page from the New York decorator Alex Papachristidis, why upholster a sofa in a single fabric when you can instead use nine—not to mention tassels?

In this chapter, you'll notice sometimes outlandish color statements, eye-catching effects, and clashing patterns and textures mixed and matched with abandon. Certainly, this is not decorating for the faint of heart. It takes a deft eye to engineer an idiosyncratic decor that works, and even the meekest among us can learn from these tour-de-force spaces. Notice the skillful use of scale in these rooms, the bravado in the color palettes, the artful deployment of large collections of objects, and the attention to the small details—from woodwork to curtain hardware to floor patterns—that can make or break any room. More than anything, be inspired to create spaces to remember—remarkable and unforgettable rooms that inhabit your flights of fancy and surround you with your dreams. Or as the legendary French antiques dealer and decorator Madeleine Castaing so memorably put it, "Be audacious, but with taste."

"I WAS DETERMINED
TO FIND THE RIGHT WAY TO
KEEP THE APARTMENT
ECLECTIC AND MAKE IT FEEL A
LITTLE COLLAGE-LIKE BY
HAVING TINY DISCOVERIES
IN EACH CORNER"

Olivier Gagnère,
designer

ABOVE: A salon in Olivier Gagnère's Paris apartment is furnished with a mix of exotic textiles, artworks, and unique furniture and objects. An oak bench holds a Pierre Charpin platter, a concrete candelabra, and ceramic vases designed by Gagnère.

RIGHT: In a Fifth Avenue apartment designed by Timothy Haynes and Kevin Roberts, the dining table of bronze, glass, and Lucite was commissioned from the Parisian designer Maria Pergay. The light fixture is vintage Lobmeyr, and the 1940s chairs are by René Drouet. The fireplace surround is made of antiqued mirrored panels and the glass moldings were originally designed by Dorothy Draper for the Hampshire House.

ABOVE: Decorator Lorenzo Castillo's Madrid home has a leafy glass-enclosed courtyard that is used as an indoor garden. The space is decorated with chaises upholstered in a Madeleine Castaing fabric and a cast of a sculpture by Michelangelo, which was found in a Paris flea market. The Gothic Revival doors are 19th-century Spanish.

LEFT: Todd and Amy Hase's home in Water Mill, New York, has a guest room furnished with a Qing dynasty wedding bed.

FACING PAGE: In decorator Martyn Lawrence Bullard's Los Angeles villa, a Fortuny fabric inspired the dining room's stenciled ceiling. The light fixture is made of Indian lanterns, and 19th-century Italian chairs surround a custom-made table.

Antiques dealer Liza Sherman remade the living area of her midtown Manhattan apartment by knocking down walls and applying strategic doses of paint, from the bright yellow on the floor to the swath of black paint above and below the windows. The quirky decor includes a light fixture of hand-blown glass bubbles, an Italian carved-wood daybed upholstered in burlap, and a Hollywood stage light.

FACING PAGE: In the apartment he shares with Scott Nelson, decorator Alex Papachristidis created a velvet-walled library with étagères overlaid in wool felt. The lampshades are trimmed in batik tablecloths, and the sofa is covered in nine different fabrics.

RIGHT: In Jackie Astier's New York dining room, a 19th-century French chandelier hangs above a dining table made from a pair of 1970s brass bases that she found on eBay. The dining chairs are 1940s French, and the rug is by The Rug Company.

WHAT THE PROS KNOW: *FEARLESS COLOR*

MORE THE MERRIER

If a little color can loosen up a space, a lot of color can be absolutely liberating. "A limited palette would limit the amount of things I can put in here," says decorator Alex Papachristidis of his art- and object-crammed Manhattan apartment. In his library, opposite, the color scheme consists of a jewel box of shades: reds, oranges, purples, yellows, blues, and golds.

DARK'S DRAMA

A dark wall color can ground a room that contains many disparate elements. In interior designer Gwynn Griffith's San Antonio home on page 95, a former factory, the living room's soaring walls are painted tobacco-brown as a backdrop to the dozens of paintings of assorted sizes and styles that climb from floor to ceiling.

SHINE ON

To pull off a gutsy color, get a good paint job. The gleaming walls in stylist Jackie Astier's New York dining room, above, resemble the night sky—an effect that she pulled off by having the walls coated in no less than ten coats of pitch-black lacquer.

BOLD CHOICE

A single knockout color can be all a room needs to make it soar. Choose shades that are unexpected: In her dining room in Athens, Georgia, on page 88, artist Susan Hable Smith covered the walls in psychedelic-patterned wallpaper in hot pink—a brazen choice that, paired with a matching rug, transforms this otherwise demure space into a bombshell.

COOL DOWN

A subtle palette of light or neutral shades can be effective in a space where the emphasis is on other elements, such as sparkle or texture. For instance, in a New York apartment designed by Timothy Haynes and Kevin Roberts on pages 74–75, silvered wallpaper lends a cool shimmer to a room where the eye candy consists of antiqued mirror panels, glass fireplace moldings, and a vintage crystal chandelier.

ABOVE: The loggia at Kelly Behun's weekend home in Long Island, New York, has floor-to-ceiling glass walls that open to face the Atlantic Ocean. The rope stool and blue chair are by Christian Astuguevieille, the wicker stools are by IKEA, and Behun designed the table with its mosaic-tile base and Macassar ebony top.

LEFT: In cosmetics executive John Demsey's Manhattan townhouse, the breakfast area has kitchen-themed Clarence House wallpaper and a friend's sketches of the homeowner. The Saarinen Tulip table and chairs are by Knoll.

FACING PAGE: For a client's London apartment, Alex Papachristidis designed a luxurious master bedroom with a 1940s vanity, Samuel Marx mirror, silk curtains, and crystal drops by sculptor Rob Wynne mounted on the wall. The plaster stool is by John Dickinson.

The dining room in Alexis and Trevor Traina's San Francisco townhouse—decorated with Thomas Britt and Ann Getty—includes such whimsical touches as a Venetian grotto table and chairs that once belonged to Franco Zeffirelli. The room faces a garden designed by Madison Cox. The artworks are by Joel Meyerowitz and Tina Barney.

FACING PAGE, TOP: Born in Algeria, Gérard Tremolet created a guest room in his Normandy château inspired by the Oriental rooms he remembered from his childhood in North Africa. The space has purple-, red-, and orange-striped walls, leopard print chairs, and a Venetian cabinet.

FACING PAGE, BOTTOM LEFT: In a client's London home, Alex Papachristidis furnished a guest room with twin beds of his design and a John Dickinson table of galvanized metal.

FACING PAGE, BOTTOM RIGHT: The walls of the master bath in Mehall Griffey and Jerry Maggi's apartment in Catania, Italy, are covered in green and gold Bisazza tile. The French mirror is 1950s, and the custom sink was handmade by Sicilian craftsmen.

ABOVE: A painted concrete staircase, slightly Surrealist in appearance, ascends in French fashion designer Yvan Mispelaere's unconventional Paris apartment, which he designed with architect Stéphane Ghestem.

"IF YOU MIX PATTERN AND
COLOR WELL, YOU
CAN GET AN INCREDIBLE SENSE
OF DEPTH THAT IS
INTERESTING FOREVER"

Alex Papachristidis,
interior designer

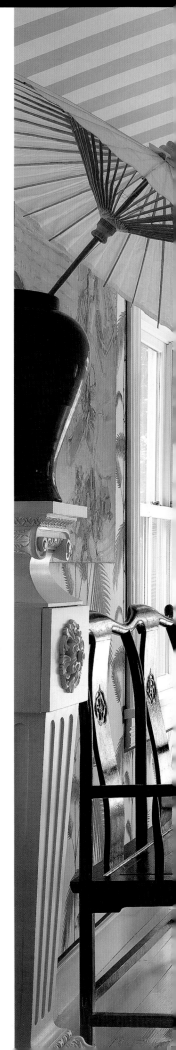

ABOVE: Susan Hable Smith's dining room in Athens, Georgia, is covered in hot-pink wallpaper in a psychedelic print, which she brought back from London. The chairs, table, and walnut chest are all antique, as is the portrait. The photograph is by the Athens-based photographer Rinne Allen and the rug is Scandinavian.

RIGHT: The entry to fashion executive Erika Bearman's Southampton, New York, home—which was decorated by Miles Redd—has a turquoise-and-white striped ceiling meant to recall the cabanas at her favorite Harbour Island hotel. The antique bench and console are Chinese, and the wallpaper is by Lee Jofa.

ANATOMY OF A ROOM

This New York apartment's study is wrapped in boiseries, or wood paneling, that was hand-made in France. It's an 18th-century look, but decorator Robert Couturier's decision to paint the panels in vivid hues makes the room feel contemporary and fresh.

- **ORANGE CRUSH** The homeowner asked her decorator for bright colors that would contrast with the traditional paneling. "I wanted the colors to be pure—no muted taupe variations," she says. The study's orange was inspired by the hue of an Hermès box.

- **BY CONTRAST** Couturier grounds the orange by using neutral colors—white, cream, and dark brown—to frame and control the brighter hue on the wall's panels, as well as for piping and seat backs on a pair of painted-wood Louis XVI chairs.

- **TIME TRAVEL** The room's eclectic mix also keeps the space from feeling stuffy. Couturier combines 18th-century antiques with a Jean Royère chandelier from the 1950s, a 1980s floor lamp, and a 1990s cocktail table by Garouste & Bonetti. The carefully controlled color scheme helps the decade-hopping decor to coalesce.

- **CURVES AHEAD** Couturier uses the room's odd shape to advantage by creating a mix of recti-linear and rounded shapes. The wall paneling and parquet floors endow the space with a graphic structure, while a demilune sofa and round cocktail table and the dramatic arc of the floor lamp add sinuousness and a sense of comfort and even whimsy.

TOP: Alexis and Trevor Traina's master bedroom in San Francisco marries a traditional aesthetic with high-octane touches, mixing a magenta-and-white toile de Jouy with a wrought-iron bed and window valances designed by Andrew Fisher, who once worked with Tony Duquette. To heighten the color quotient, designer Ann Getty added lilac stools and yellow-and-white bedding.

CENTER: At fashion designer Carlos Miele's beach house in Brazil, the pool extends into the living area. The hanging chair is by Armando Cerello.

BOTTOM: For a family home in Tuxedo Park, New York, decorator Jeffrey Bilhuber created a playful club room designed for game nights (bridge in particular). The furnishings include card tables, French bistro chairs, and Lars Bolander umbrellas.

FACING PAGE: The walls of the kitchen in Leslie and Sean Goodrich's Manhattan apartment, decorated by Muriel Brandolini, are sheathed in blue felt and embroidered with hand-beaded lyrics from Lou Reed's song "Perfect Day." The table is by Piet Hein Eek.

"I'M A RESTLESS SPIRIT. I LOVE
CHANGE. I'VE BEEN KNOWN TO MOVE THE BED
TO THE MIDDLE OF THE LIVING
ROOM IF THE MOOD STRIKES. NOTHING
IS NAILED DOWN"

Gwynn Griffith, decorator

FACING PAGE: Jean-Louis Deniot created a grand double-height central staircase foyer in Nasreen and Moin Qureshi's home in New Delhi, India. The entry hall features a 38-foot-high ceiling, a sweeping balustrade, and geometrically patterned floors and walls that were crafted from local marbles.

ABOVE: Gwynn Griffith's art-filled living room in a former factory in San Antonio, Texas, features a John Dickinson plaster table, a wicker tub chair covered with a shearling throw, and a French chandelier. The paintings include some of Griffith's own, as well as the work of her sons, Sam Giesey and Greg Mannino.

Alexis and Trevor Traina's San Francisco living room, decorated by Thomas Britt, has walls, curtains, and sofa upholstery in a claret-color, hand-blocked velvet by Sabina Fay Braxton. Britt designed the bone-inlaid tables, and the artworks are by Hiroshi Sugimoto, John Baldessari, and Jackie Nickerson.

ABOVE: The guest room mural in Maryam Montague and Chris Redecke's home near Marrakesh, was inspired by a screen made by Armand Albert Rateau. The quilt is Indian, the Moroccan chairs are covered in mud cloth from Mali, and a vintage Moroccan rug covers the floor.

RIGHT: In Leslie and Sean Goodrich's Manhattan apartment, decorator Muriel Brandolini had a dramatic *lit à la polonaise* canopy bed custom-made in France for the couple's master bedroom, in what was formerly the living room. The patterned wool rug is by Fedora Design.

WHAT THE PROS KNOW: *SHOWSTOPPERS*

HANDCRAFTED

The most unique decor isn't generally available off the shelf. Seek out artisans who can help to create eye-catching elements, whether it's one-of-a-kind woodwork, an iron stair rail, a spectacular set of curtains, or bespoke hardware.

MIX MASTER

Don't be afraid to combine wildly different fabric patterns in the same room. Brazilian style setter Fabrizio Rollo shows how effective this visual device can be in his living room, below, where he mixes ethnic textiles, vintage leopard prints, green velvet, and white linen. The trick is to pair patterns that contrast in scale—in Rollo's home, the large-scale geometric motif of a suzani throw is balanced by the smaller repeating pattern of the leopard. Or try pairing a large graphic print with a delicate floral.

EN MASSE

Turn a collection of objects into a room's focal point. In Paris, fashion designer Andrew Gn created a red-walled room as the backdrop for his collection of blue-and-white Chinese porcelain and faience plates and urns, which are mounted en masse on the walls and on shelves, page 104.

STAND OUT

Design a room around an architectural showpiece. In Prince Emanuele Filiberto di Savoia's home on Lake Geneva, the living room is furnished with a semicircular sofa that faces a dramatic fireplace shaped like the mouth of a fish on pages 106–107.

THIS AND THAT

Try pairing quirky elements with more traditional ones. In the Madrid sitting room of Lorenzo Castillo, on page 70, the decorative elements careen from the eccentric (a steel-and-ostrich-egg mirror, a Rubik's Cube–like artwork) to the classic (a Jacob Frères armchair, a diamond-patterned marble floor).

GO FAUX

Trompe l'oeil is a mainstay of the fanciful room, from faux-sky ceilings to murals of faraway scenes. New technologies such as digital printing make almost anything possible. In his oak-paneled library in Paris, opposite, Parisian designer Jean-Louis Deniot inserted sections of canvas that were laser-printed to resemble tree bark.

LEFT: Brazilian editor and trendsetter Fabrizio Rollo furnished his living room in São Paulo with a daybed and pillow covered in a vintage leopard-print fabric by Madeleine Castaing. The Bertoia chair is topped with a Lesage embroidered pillow. A chair designed by Rollo is upholstered in a Ralph Lauren linen.

FACING PAGE: An 18th-century portrait hangs in the library of Jean-Louis Deniot's Paris apartment. A vintage Gio Ponti chair is paired with a Jacques Adnet desk and a C. Jere lamp. Deniot designed the rug and sofa.

LEFT: No surface is left unembellished in this garden-themed dressing room in Alex Papachristidis and Scott Nelson's Manhattan apartment. The walls, sofa, draperies and even the lampshades are all covered in exuberant florals.

ABOVE: The kitchen in fashion designer Liza Bruce and Nicholas Alvis Vega's home outside Marrakesh has Berber mud walls and was built around a tree that now grows through its roof. The counters and floor tiles were locally crafted, the low kitchen cabinets are fitted with Musharabi screens, and the Berber-style ceiling was constructed out of reeds and wood beams.

ABOVE: With its chinoiserie wallpaper, glossy black furniture, and taxidermy peacock, the study in Anna Sui's Manhattan apartment—which she designed with Mani Colaku—reflects the fashion designer's funky style. The busts are by Gemma Taccogna.

RIGHT: In Paris, fashion designer Andrew Gn displays a mix of European and Chinese porcelains and faience in his red "porcelain room." Both the Swedish tea table and the Italian chest are 18th century.

FACING PAGE: The dramatic entry hall in Lara and Jeff Sanderson's home on Mercer Island, Washington, which was decorated by Kelly Wearstler, has a painted striped ceiling, a floor patterned in three different marbles, and a brass-railed staircase.

The living room in Geneva, Switzerland, of Prince Emanuele Filiberto di Savoia—which was designed in the 1970s by his mother, Marina, Princess of Naples, with architect Jacques Lopez—contains a semicircular pleated-silk sofa and a fireplace shaped like the mouth of a fish. The marble-and-metal flower tables are custom-made and the lamps are by Gae Aulenti. A painting of the Italian royal family hangs above the fireplace.

"I DON'T HAVE ANY FEAR
ABOUT MIXING
EVERYTHING. IN BRAZIL, THERE IS
ONE ROOM IN MY HOUSE
WITH FIVE HUNDRED PIECES
OF FABRIC"

Sig Bergamin, interior designer

ABOVE: The living room in the Manhattan apartment of São Paulo–based designer Sig Bergamin features an exuberant mix of colors, prints, and styles. The curtains are of a Georges Le Manach cotton and the walls are sheathed in a Braquenié fabric. The dhurrie is Indian, and the photograph of Gisele Bündchen is by Michel Comte.

RIGHT: Liza Bruce and Nicholas Alvis Vega painted the sitting room of their Moroccan villa hot pink. The room is furnished with furniture and objects from their travels, ranging from a 1940s Yoruba armchair to a carved-wood Ethiopian chair. Vega designed the fireplace surround based on the Moroccan eight-pointed-star motif.

TOP: Brazilian style editor Fabrizio Rollo furnished his guest room with a silk canopy by Safira Sedas, an ikat throw from Istanbul's Grand Bazaar, and a painted table from the 1940s. The walls are decorated with framed Christian Dior scarves and sketches for Meissen porcelain.

RIGHT: In Maryam Montague and Chris Redecke's Moroccan home, the 1960s sofa in the library is covered with a suzani from Kyrgyzstan. The tables are made from Moroccan road signs, and a vintage wool blanket serves as a rug.

FACING PAGE: In her home in a converted factory in San Antonio, Texas, designer Gwynn Griffith fashioned a great room with soaring ceilings and black painted floors. In this atmospheric and art-filled space, an antique Italian table is stacked with books.

Woman in the Mirror Richard Avedon

Christian Dior

ANATOMY OF A ROOM

With its deep teal walls and ethnic textiles, the master bedroom in fashion editor Kim Hersov's London townhouse feels like an exotic and intensely private retreat. The atmosphere is both old-world and of the moment.

- **HIGH TOP** The custom-made four-poster bed has a canopy that reaches almost to the ceiling, an effect that both accentuates the height of the space and makes this sizable room feel cozier. The bed walks the line between traditional and modern: Its turned legs have classic details, but the canopy frame (and lack of side panels) feels contemporary. With its black lacquered finish, the four-poster has a clean, graphic style that grounds the room's colorful and multilayered decor.

- **WRITE STUFF** Instead of side tables, Hersov had the clever idea of flanking the bed with a pair of small vintage desks that came out of a Madrid jewelry store. They work beautifully as bedside tables, but with the addition of lamps and bamboo chairs (she discovered the latter at a Paris flea market) the desks also function as fully equipped writing desks.

- **SING THE BLUES** The walls are covered in a deep teal silk. The dark, enveloping wall color adds richness to the bedroom and a sense of mystery. Hersov deepened the effect by layering in a rug in the same tone, and by adding a range of patterned blue textiles, including the bed's striking paisley throw.

- **SCREEN STARS** Blue creates the drama in this master bedroom, but blue's complement—yellow, in the form of gold—helps warm up the moody space. Gold silk curtains hang from floor to ceiling and increase the bedroom's glamour quotient. Meanwhile, a dramatic pair of gold-and-black screens gleams in the corners behind the bed.

PRACTICAL

Not so very long ago, the functional rooms in a home were hidden out of sight. From kitchens to bathrooms, these practical spaces were decorated in a no-nonsense utilitarian style—think subway tile long before it was chic, and laundry rooms concealed in the basement. In those days, few homeowners would have even considered installing handmade designer tile in a kitchen or bath, let alone encasing a kitchen's cabinetry in black crocodile-stamped leather panels crafted by artisans who work for Louis Vuitton.

How times have changed. Once overlooked, practical spaces are the new trophy rooms. Like many good things, this trend started in the kitchen, which has gradually pushed beyond its galley walls to become the heart of the home. Today, kitchens have become a vehicle for self-expression. Even when it is small, it is a focal point, with decor to match. From rich materials to state-of-the-art appliances, fine art to chandeliers, anything goes in today's kitchens. They set the stage for modern life. More than just cooking spaces, they are the rooms where everyone congregates—a setting for everything from after-school homework sessions to convivial dinner parties where hanging out with the cook (and offering to chop a few vegetables) is part of the evening's fun.

Bathrooms, too, have expanded in size to become places where we love to unwind. The more we travel to luxury hotels and spas, the more we seem to want to bring the look back home—or even surpass it. In this section, we visit a wide range of bathrooms, from Cameron Diaz's jewel box of a guest bath in pink onyx and brass, seen on page 142, to Ralph Lauren's sleek white marble and mirrored space overlooking Central Park on pages 160–161.

Of course, baths and kitchens aren't the only practical spaces where form and function coexist in equal measure. As the entry halls from such interior designers as Miles Redd (page 168) and Steven Gambrel (page 117) demonstrate, nothing sets the tone for a home better than an eye-catching vestibule. And at a moment when more of us are working at home, the elegant home offices by decorators Sara Story and Bunny Williams (pages 134 and 138–139) would certainly make any task seem more pleasant.

From Sandra Lee's chic home gym, complete with a portrait of Jim Morrison (page 159), to a range of colorful (and blissfully well-organized) children's rooms by such A-list designers as Sheila Bridges and Steven Volpe (pages 126 and 135), these practical spaces are proof that even the hardest-working rooms in our homes need not skimp on style.

"KITCHENS MAKE ME
UNCOMFORTABLE. I DON'T COOK, SO I
WANT IT TO BE LIKE ANOTHER
ROOM. I WANT TO BE ENTERTAINED. I WANT
THINGS TO LOOK AT"

Robert Duffy, homeowner

LEFT: The vibrant kitchen in Marc Jacobs executive Robert Duffy's Provincetown home—designed by architect Stephan Jaklitsch and decorator Richard McGeehan—has a yellow Aga stove, an antique Belgian butcher's table, and vintage pendant lights. Clarice Cliff pottery is displayed on the open shelving.

FACING PAGE: A dazzling 1960s Italian mirror with a frame of hand-carved loops is the focal point in a Manhattan foyer designed by Steven Gambrel; the walls are Venetian plaster, and the graphic black-and-white floor is marble.

PAGE 114: French furniture designer Christian Liaigre created this serene all-white guest bathroom in his vacation home on the island of St. Barts. Local craftsmen made the shelves and steel-frame mirror, and the floor is of local stone.

LEFT: In the Notting Hill townhouse he shares with his partner, Sebastian Scott, decorator Peter Mikic created a master bathroom that is furnished like a salon, complete with a custom sofa, rug, and silk wall covering. The chest of drawers and mirror are 19th century, and the freestanding tub is antique.

ABOVE: Decorator Martyn Lawrence Bullard turned a guest room in his Los Angeles house into a 300-square-foot dressing room. The space is furnished with red cabinetry, a cedar-lined cupboard for cashmeres, and walls covered in a hand-loomed ikat fabric that Bullard designed for Schumacher.

Architect Gil Schafer and decorator Miles Redd collaborated on the design of this expansive and high-ceilinged kitchen in a Greek Revival–inspired home in upstate New York. The cabinets are custom-made, and the 19th-century chairs are upholstered in a Bennison linen.

LEFT: In a traditional Nantucket shingled house, architect Rebecca Ascher created a light-filled master bath with a contemporary feel. The Victoria + Albert freestanding bathtub is made of volcanic limestone and resin.

BELOW: The kitchen of Allison and Robby Adams's home in Tampa, Florida, which was designed by Nate Berkus, is fitted with teak counters, marble wall tiles, and stainless-steel cabinetry with brass knobs. The stools are by BDDW and the light fixtures are by Historical Materialism.

FACING PAGE: In a 1857 Manhattan townhouse near Gramercy Park designed by Sheila Bridges, the dining room has a 19th-century Spanish chandelier and a custom-made wine-tasting table. French cabinets from the 19th century flank the original Victorian marble mantel.

FACING PAGE: Decorator Kelly Wearstler created a jewel box of a kitchen for the actress Cameron Diaz in her Manhattan apartment. The backsplash, counters, and sink fittings are unlacquered brass. The wood floors were treated with an ebony stain and then cerused.

LEFT: The French-inspired kitchen in the Hamptons house of furniture designers Amy and Todd Hase is furnished with an 18th-century table from a Paris flea market. The light fixture is from Circa Lighting and the range, vent hood, and dishwasher are by Viking.

WHAT THE PROS KNOW: *KITCHENS*

COLOR CODE

While white always looks right in a kitchen, these days it is no longer the only option. In a kitchen in Mercer Island, Washington, designed by Kelly Wearstler, on page 137, a brass island and cerused oak cabinetry combine with black marble and ebonized floors. On page 134, Nathan Turner's kitchen floor is painted in a Farrow & Ball hue called Arsenic.

MATERIAL CONNECTION

The range of surface materials available for kitchens has never been wider, from such classic choices as marble and tile to newer options like Corian and quartz. While many surfaces are trouble-free, materials such as stone need regular sealing—or not. Wear and tear can add patina.

"I like that the counters show every water ring and squeeze of lemon juice," says the actress Cameron Diaz of her kitchen's unsealed brass countertops, opposite. "They give the place soul."

THE RIGHT LIGHT

Good lighting is essential in any kitchen, from task lighting over working surfaces to mood lighting on dimmer switches in dining areas. Paolo Moschino's London kitchen on page 157 features runway-style lights over the kitchen island, while a row of pendant lamps provide softer illumination over the breakfast table.

APPLIANCE OPTIONS

Whatever your need, there is an appliance to fulfill it—from wine refrigerators to pizza ovens, any culinary desire can be addressed in today's home kitchens. Stainless-steel appliances are a modern classic, but color is an increasingly popular option—from Amy and Todd Hase's cobalt Viking stove, above, to Robert Duffy's classic Aga range in bright yellow, page 116.

FINE DETAILS

Don't hesitate to personalize a kitchen with unique details, personal items, even artwork. Ellen DeGeneres incorporates one-of-a-kind antiques like a 19th-century Swedish chalkboard and an old baker's rack in her kitchen on page 126. In a home in Tampa, on page 122, decorator Nate Berkus fitted the stainless-steel cabinetry with brass knobs, a combination that recalls a Rolex watch.

ABOVE: In the kitchen area of one of several buildings on the ranch of Ellen DeGeneres and Portia de Rossi, which was decorated by Cliff Fong, a 19th-century Swedish chalkboard hangs above a 1900 French bluestone-top table. The baker's rack is an antique.

LEFT: In a New York townhouse decorated by Sheila Bridges, the son's room is painted in Farrow & Ball's Cook's Blue, and furnished with a BDDW chair, a Ducduc desk, and a Stark rug. The artwork includes, from left, prints by Selma Bortner and Roy Lichtenstein, a painting by a friend, and a Jackson Pollock–inspired painting by a family member.

FACING PAGE: The bathroom in hotelier Costis Psychas's home on the island of Therassia in Greece features walls and arches made of plaster that was built up by hand and finished with a fresco technique, in the manner of Santorini's traditional cave houses. A friend made the wood boat in the corner.

"I DO LOVE BLACK. IT CREATES
CONTRAST. RATHER THAN
MAKING A SPACE FEEL SMALLER, AS YOU MIGHT
EXPECT, IT HELPS TO DEFINE
ITS OUTER EDGES, ENCOURAGING
VISUAL SCALE"

Steven Gambrel, decorator

FACING PAGE: A kitchen in the Hamptons designed by Steven Gambrel features glazed ebony ceramic tile from a firm that once supplied them to fire stations. The floor is gray, black, and white French concrete tiles that are laid to give an Op Art look.

ABOVE: In a palazzo in Catania, on the Italian island of Sicily, owners Mehall Griffey and Jerry Maggi worked with their painter to create the perfect blood orange shade for the guest bath. The room has 19th-century reclaimed Sicilian wall tiles and a Devon & Devon tub.

ABOVE: Alix and Bruno Verney's Brussels kitchen, designed by architect Frédéric Haesevoets, has a polished resin floor and a 13-foot-long white island by Bulthaup. The vent hood is by AEG, the stools are by E15, and the hanging light fixtures are by Ionna Vautrin. The artworks include an almost life-size Don Brown statue of his wife, Yoko.

FACING PAGE: The foyer of Tina and Jeffrey Bolton's Manhattan apartment, which was designed by John Saladino, has walls of scratch-coat plaster and Louis XVI oak doors. The entry table is by Dennis & Leen, the spoon-back chairs are by Saladino Furniture, and the portrait of a woman is by Ellen Emmet Rand.

ANATOMY OF A ROOM

This striking Hamptons kitchen is as eye-catching as it is hardworking—no surprise since it belongs to chef and Food Network star Bobby Flay and actress Stephanie March, his wife. Flay presided over the design of the restaurant-caliber kitchen he had always dreamed of having at home.

- **HIGH VELOCITY** As a professional chef, Flay is accustomed to cooking on the best equipment and wanted the same at home. His kitchen has a ten-burner stove, two ovens, a fryer, a griddle, and a salamander (a restaurant-caliber broiler). "I love that my [home] kitchen is technically a restaurant," he says.

- **ISLAND DREAMS** A long kitchen island anchors the room and provides Flay with a stage of sorts: He can use the marble counter as a work space while Stephanie and their friends keep him company. It's no busman's holiday: Flay genuinely loves to cook and socialize in his free time on weekends. "I stand at my kitchen island from the minute I get out here to the minute I leave," Flay says.

- **TRUE BLUE** The kitchen's design features an intriguing mix of textures, from the tile floor to the slate backsplash and metal accents such as the brass pendants. But it is the striking teal color of the cabinets and island (Benjamin Moore's almost-tropical Majestic Blue) that really adds verve to the space.

- **ALL WELCOME** The kitchen features plenty of seating for friends, including two café tables with French bistro chairs, an island with metal Tolix H stools, and, in an adjacent space, a long farm table. At the previous Thanksgiving, he says, "We had fifty people show up for turkey in Amagansett. They followed us out here!"

ABOVE: Decorator Sara Story converted an entry hall in her Manhattan apartment into a cozy home office. The wallpaper is from de Gournay, the Parsons desk is by West Elm, and the chair is by Eames.

LEFT: In a Malibu apartment they nicknamed the Boat House, decorators Nathan Turner and Eric Hughes created a shiplike kitchen that takes advantage of every square inch. The cabinetry is by SieMatic and the floor is painted in Farrow & Ball's Arsenic.

FACING PAGE: For Bita Daryabari's son's room in London, decorator Steven Volpe's bold red-and-blue design scheme includes a pair of custom-designed beds, a Tom Dixon bookcase, and a print by Rodney Graham.

FACING PAGE: In the entrance hall of his Manhattan apartment, decorator Alex Papachristidis covered the walls and ceiling in a variegated-stripe linen by Lee Jofa, to create the effect of a tent. The parrot print is by Walton Ford.

ABOVE: In a home in the Hamptons, designer Steven Gambrel outfitted a master dressing room with a goatskin rug, vintage Maison Charles lanterns, and floor-to-ceiling cabinets painted high-gloss white with red trim.

RIGHT: Lara and Jeff Sanderson's kitchen in Mercer Island, Washington, which was decorated by Kelly Wearstler, has a brass island, cerused oak cabinetry, and marble countertops.

In a New York penthouse apartment, decorator Bunny Williams furnished the entrance to the study with a pair of early-19th-century American fluted columns. The desk lamp and Moroccan rug are vintage, and the stool is by Jules-Émile Leleu. The floors are honed pink granite and the walls are mica-flecked plaster.

WHAT THE PROS KNOW: *DRESSING ROOMS*

MADE TO MEASURE

Before outfitting a closet with cabinetry, take an inventory of what you have and position shelves and rods to take advantage of the space. In a closet designed by Celerie Kemble, opposite, the homeowner determined the number of her handbags, the heights of her boots, and the hanging measurement of both her and her husband's clothing. The resulting dressing room fits the couple to a T.

ISLAND DREAMS

If you have the space, an island equipped with drawers can take the place of a dresser, and the top surface is helpful for laying out outfits. On page 119, Martyn Lawrence Bullard's gentleman's wardrobe (formerly a 300-square-foot guest room) has red cabinetry, including an island as well as a cedar-lined cupboard for cashmeres.

ROOM FOR LIVING

A dressing room can be a multipurpose space: Some incorporate bathtubs, showers, or even small work spaces. On page 148, in a Manhattan apartment designed by Timothy Haynes and Kevin Roberts, the dressing room has a Jansen desk and chair that complement the chic decor, and serve as the homeowner's home office.

DECORATIVE TOUCH

From chandeliers to wallpaper and armchairs, homeowners are embellishing their dressing rooms with beautiful decorative elements that wouldn't look out of place anywhere in the home. Aerin Lauder's jewel box of a dressing room, below, has hand-painted floral wallpaper, a vintage Gabriella Crespi veneered brass desk, and a Baguès crystal chandelier.

LEFT: The traditional design of Aerin Lauder's Manhattan dressing room was created by the French interior designer Jacques Grange. The painted wallpaper is by Gracie.

FACING PAGE: In the dressing room of Jane and Michael DeFlorio's Manhattan townhouse, which was designed by Celerie Kemble, a central marble-topped island with drawers takes the place of a dresser. The room, gleaming in high-sheen lacquer, has a brass chandelier by Alexa Hampton for Visual Comfort and a painting by André Dunoyer de Segonzac.

ABOVE: In the guest bath of Cameron Diaz's Manhattan apartment, which was designed by Kelly Wearstler, the vanity top and walls are pink onyx, the sink is brass, the vintage sconces are French, and the shower stall is custom-made.

RIGHT: The home office in decorator Paula Caravelli's Manhattan apartment has a collage made of black-and-white images by Robert Greene, circa-1845 klismos chairs from Denmark, and a custom-made black laminate desk.

"I CAN WAX ON
AND ON ABOUT THE UTILITY OF
A NEUTRAL PALETTE.
IT'S PARTICULARLY HELPFUL
FOR PEOPLE STARTING
OUT WITH THEIR FIRST APARTMENT
OR HOUSE. YOU CAN MOVE
THINGS FROM ROOM TO ROOM
MORE EASILY"

Darryl Carter, interior designer

LEFT: Decorator Darryl Carter's Washington, D.C., townhouse kitchen has a pared-down palette and is furnished with an antique Italian étagère and granite countertops. French doors lead to the sunny breakfast room at the back of the house.

ABOVE: Bita Daryabari's London bathroom, decorated by Steven Volpe, has walls sheathed in Calacatta marble and floors that combine Jerusalem stone and marble.

ABOVE: The children's room in Winsome Brown and Claude Arpels's New York loft, which was designed by architect Lee Mindel, is furnished with custom-made bunk beds, IKEA bedding, and a table and chair by Alvar Aalto.

LEFT: Designer Mark Cunningham created a dark-walled library in Manhattan for the model Hana Soukupova and her husband, Drew Aaron. The vintage metal-and-Lucite chandelier is by Maison Charles, the oak desk chairs are by André Sornay, and the red painted-steel sculpture is by Alexander Liberman.

FACING PAGE: For a kitchen in California designed by M. Elle Design and architect Bob White of ForestStudio, the built-in banquette was upholstered in linen. The table is custom-made and the armchairs are by Lucca Studio. The beams and ceiling are of reclaimed barn wood.

ABOVE: An underused dining room was reborn as a cozy library in Julie Anne Quay's Manhattan apartment, which was designed by Richard Mishaan. The room has grass-cloth-covered walls, plush seating, and a luminous gold-leaf ceiling.

LEFT: Architects Rebecca Ascher and Joshua Davis furnished this contemporary kitchen in Nantucket with a Corian-top island and ash-veneer cabinets. The stools are by Samare and the vent hood is by Abbaka. The wood floor, Ascher says, "has a slightly beaten look, to go with the sand-duney nature of the site."

FACING PAGE: In a Fifth Avenue apartment in Manhattan designed by Timothy Haynes and Kevin Roberts, the woman's dressing room has lavender lacquered cabinetry, a Jansen desk, and bird's-eye views of neighboring rooftops. The Lobmeyr chandelier is from the 1960s, and the stools are by Silas Seandel.

ABOVE: The dining area of fashion designer Carlos Miele's midcentury-inspired Brazilian beach house has a table from southeastern Brazil and handcrafted bamboo chairs. The bench on the terrace is carved out of pequi wood, and the large photographs are of a performance Miele staged at the Kennedy Center.

CENTER: The minimalist kitchen in Monica Mandelli and Marco Valla's Manhattan apartment, which was designed by Bruce T. Bananto, features Varenna Poliform cabinetry, CaesarStone counters, and a Viking cooktop. Bright yellow Le Creuset cookware, along with wood floors, lends warmth to the white and stainless-steel space.

LEFT: Designer Richard Mishaan used a narrow green border as a design motif in Julie Anne Quay's Manhattan kitchen, which is furnished with an Eero Saarinen Tulip table for Knoll and Philippe Starck chairs for Kartell.

FACING PAGE: The master bath in a Manhattan apartment designed by Daniel Romualdez sports acid-etched-glass walls, marble floors, and a custom bench. The sculptural bathtub is by Waterworks.

In designer Olivier Gagnère's Paris apartment, the small kitchen opens onto the living area. A pendant light with a cardboard shade hangs over a table draped with a Basque tablecloth, and the sofa is topped with an antique suzani from Afghanistan. Gagnère designed the vinyl and enameled-glass cocktail table.

ABOVE: In a master bath in the Hamptons designed by Steven Gambrel, the vanities are modeled on those at Claridge's, the homeowner's favorite London hotel. The shower walls and floor are travertine, and the sconces are by Jacques Adnet.

RIGHT: In the dressing room of television producer Ellen Rakieten's Chicago apartment, which was designed by Nate Berkus and Anne Coyle, a vintage Baguès chandelier hangs over a Poillerat-style table. Vintage ostrich-egg lamps flank a painting by James Brown.

"IN ITALY, YOU MIGHT HAVE A
BIG PALAZZO, BUT YOU SERVE MOZZARELLA
AND TOMATOES FOR LUNCH. IT'S A
RELAXED APPROACH WITHIN THE HISTORICAL
GRANDEUR OF A ROOM"

Paolo Moschino, interior designer

ABOVE: In London, Paolo Moschino
and the architecture firm Tyler Mandic
designed a contemporary kitchen for
Sofia and Niccolo Barattieri di San Pietro
in what was previously a living room.
Runway-style lights hang above
the custom cabinetry, which is framed
in marble. The photographs are by
Montserrat Soto.

LEFT: Decorator Darryl Carter's master
bath in Washington, D.C., is furnished
with architectural fragments and a pair of
bathtubs salvaged from the Russian
embassy. Carter designed the shutters.
The secretary is 18th century.

TOP: The kitchen in Jean-Louis Deniot's Paris apartment has cabinetry in hammered silver made in Morocco. The countertops and floor utilize four types of marble. The brass-and-opaline light fixture is by Stilnovo.

LEFT: The master bath in Alice Childress and Christopher Daniels's Manhattan loft, decorated with the help of his sister Courtnay Daniels, is furnished with an antique tub, a vintage Italian chandelier, and an 18th-century painting.

FACING PAGE, TOP LEFT: In Deniot's master bath, the cabinetry is painted to mimic the plaster-fluted walls. Felix Agostini sconces flank the custom-made medicine cabinet.

FACING PAGE, TOP RIGHT: Fashion editor Kim Hersov's London kitchen, which was designed by Hubert Zandberg, has a console and sconces made from metal bins. A light fixture from a French factory hangs above the stainless-steel island, and the barstools were found at a Paris flea market.

FACING PAGE, BOTTOM LEFT: The kitchen in the Robert Couturier-designed Manhattan duplex of celebrity hairstylist Frédéric Fekkai and his wife, Shirin von Wulffen, has a wall of custom-made Shaker-inspired cabinetry.

FACING PAGE, BOTTOM RIGHT: A rock 'n' roll spirit prevails in the exercise room of television star Sandra Lee's Westchester, New York, Colonial home. She furnished the space with shelving by California Closets and a portrait of Jim Morrison by Russell Young.

LEFT: A floor-to-ceiling window frames the view of Central Park in Ralph and Ricky Lauren's Manhattan apartment. The bath has mirrored and white-lacquered cabinetry and a Thassos marble countertop and floor.

ABOVE: In the master bedroom of her home in the mountains of Aspen, Colorado, interior designer Charlotte Moss oriented an antique architect's table to face the breathtaking alpine view.

ABOVE: In Lisa Pomerantz and Jonathan Copplestone's Manhattan apartment, which was designed by architect Peter Pawlak, a son's room has a vintage Swan sofa by Arne Jacobsen and a Tibetan rug. The mural is a Maharam wallpaper by Casey Reas.

LEFT: The red stripe in the wallpaper in a children's bath in a Manhattan townhouse designed by Sheila Bridges is echoed in the thin red line in the tile floor. A window shade in a Beacon Hill silk hangs over the claw-foot tub.

FACING PAGE: The vibrant blue study of textile designer John Robshaw's Manhattan apartment has a desk and chair by Richard Wrightman, a lamp by Brunno Jahara, and a drum shade by Broome Lampshades. The portrait and vintage rug are from India.

WHAT
THE PROS
KNOW:
BATHROOMS

FULLY FURNISHED

Today's bathrooms are decorated with the same care and attention as any room in the house. Designers are incorporating music, furniture, and even refrigerators. If not for the bathtub and sink, Peter Mikic's master bath on page 118 might be mistaken for the salon: The room is furnished with a sofa, rug, antique portrait, and silk wall coverings.

PERSONAL EXPRESSIONS

Bathrooms can feel special and personal. In her Moroccan home, below right, fashion designer Liza Bruce and her husband created a bathtub in the shape of an eight-pointed star. The room's mirrored wall treatment was based on Islamic design.

GO WILD

Powder rooms are a great place to experiment with color and pattern. Try a dramatic wall covering like the classic red and zebra-patterned Scalamandré wallpaper that decorator Miles Redd used in a small bathroom, right.

A LONG SOAK

A freestanding tub can add a sculptural element to a space. Perhaps that is why so many designers incorporate them not only into bathrooms but also into bedrooms.

MAKE ROOM

Consider turning an unused bedroom into a spacious master bath, as fashion editor Kim Hersov did in her historic London townhouse, opposite.

WARM METALS

Cool metals such as nickel and silver add a modern touch to a bath, while warmer finishes such as gold, bronze, and brass evoke old-world glamour. In Alice Childress and Christopher Daniel's SoHo loft on page 158, antique-style English fittings lend atmosphere to a room with a marble tub and a huge 18th-century painting.

FACING PAGE: Kim Hersov's master bath in London, designed by Hubert Zandberg, has a Bateau tub from the Water Monopoly.

TOP: Valerie Colas-Thibouville's powder room in Manhattan—designed by Miles Redd, Dick Bories, and James Shearron—is sheathed in Scalamandré's iconic zebra wallpaper; the sink is granite.

RIGHT: A mirrored wall treatment based on Islamic design in Liza Bruce and Nicholas Alvis Vega's home in Morocco.

The study in the Manhattan apartment of
Michael Kors executive Lisa Pomerantz and
her husband, Jonathan Copplestone, which
was designed by architect Peter Pawlak, has
a rocking chair by Robert W. Winfield that
originally belonged to her father. The room,
which opens onto a terrace, has vintage desk
lamps by Jean Prouvé and metal bookcases
by Tomas Maier for Bottega Veneta.

ABOVE: In Keith and Alina McNally's home on Martha's Vineyard, a child's room has a bed constructed of reclaimed wood.

FACING PAGE, TOP: A vintage console and a glass stool by Alison Berger serve as a work area in the living room of designers Jeffrey Alan Marks and Ross Cassidy's Santa Monica home.

FACING PAGE, BOTTOM LEFT: A colorful nursery, in a Hamptons home designed by architect Timothy Hayes and designer Kevin Roberts, has a striped Missoni carpet and a ceiling painted in pink and orange stripes. The pale pink sofa is by Jonathan Adler and the 1980s table is by Milo Baughman.

FACING PAGE, BOTTOM RIGHT: The gallery in Valerie Colas-Thibouville's Manhattan apartment, which was designed by Miles Redd, working with James Shearron and Dick Bories, was lacquered Yves Klein-blue. The leather-covered door is trimmed with silver nailheads, and the floor is painted in a faux-marble pattern.

"I LIKE TO
PUSH THE ENVELOPE—
BUT JUST
TO THE EDGE"

Miles Redd,
interior designer

"I LOVE WHAT
YOU MIGHT CALL BRUTAL
ELEGANCE, WHERE
FORM AND FUNCTION ARE
REALLY OBVIOUS"

Meg Ryan, actress

ABOVE: The master bath in actress Meg Ryan's home on Martha's Vineyard, which she decorated with Marsha Russell, has an antique earthenware tub and a mosaic floor.

RIGHT: In Malibu, designer Michael S. Smith and architect Oscar Shamamian designed a husband's bathroom with lime-washed oak paneling and a floor inset with a circa-4th-century Byzantine mosaic. The cabinet is early 19th-century Chinese.

ANATOMY OF A ROOM

The master bath in interior designer Kelly Behun's weekend house on Long Island is an object lesson in indoor-outdoor living. The room flows seamlessly into an outdoor terrace, making the most of the spectacular ocean views.

- **GO LOW** Behun's beachside home, which was designed by the architects Brian Sawyer and John Berson, is long and narrow, elegantly mirroring the ocean it faces. The furnishings, including the French limestone soaking tub and the adjacent bench located on the enclosed terrace, are also low-slung.

- **STAY CALM** The bathroom is a study in luxurious minimalism with a restrained palette that enhances the overall feeling of serenity in the space. The room's floors are of French Luget limestone, which has a warm glow like beach sand and matches the carved stone Buddha, another Zen touch.

- **CLEAR VIEW** The bathroom, like much of the house, has large windows and movable glass panel walls that seamlessly meld inside with outside. The room's elevation was carefully sited to maximize the view of the Atlantic spread beyond the dunes.

- **TOUCH OF WHIMSY** Behun, who has young children, likes to leaven her decor with light-hearted moments. In the bathroom, a shaggy-haired, goat-legged stool by sculptor Marc Bankowsky adds a dose of humor to the sleek modernism of the space.

- **WARM IT UP** Though her house is decidedly modern, Behun contrasts the clean lines with such textural elements as natural wood window frames as well as textiles. And if the weather is chilly, a funky fireplace in the sitting area keeps the room comfortable.

PERSONAL

The most fascinating people, more often than not, live in the most interesting rooms. A home that is intensely personal in spirit doesn't follow the trends. It doesn't try to be safe or attempt to keep up with the Joneses. It is the antithesis of one-stop shopping. A personal room—like a person with character—takes time to grow into itself. It's an accumulation of objects and memories that have been layered and repositioned (usually more than once) until the results feel inevitable and utterly unique.

The rooms in this chapter are all sui generis. These one-of-a-kind spaces are almost novelistic in scope, relating the narratives of their owners' histories, travels, tastes, talents, passions, and relationships. For textile designer John Robshaw, a terra-cotta wall in the living room of his Lower East Side apartment (pages 202–203) serves as a gallery both for his own artwork and for the global artisans whose work has inspired him. For fashion designer Carolina Herrera Baez, her continually evolving Madrid living room (pages 210–211) is a place to experiment with form and color.

Just like its occupants, a personal room can be artful, dramatic, outlandish, cerebral, or serene. It can be artist Susan Hable Smith's shocking-pink parlor in Athens, Georgia (page 178), or interior designer Steven Volpe's art-filled loft in San Francisco (page 208), or hotelier Costis Psychas's handcrafted retreat on a secluded island in Greece (pages 216–217). Design that reflects its owners can make a major statement: Stylist Jackie Astier's sexy library, for instance, is furnished with an eleven-foot velvet chesterfield (pages 206–207). Or a unique space might speak in quieter tones, like Linda Zelenko's New England farmhouse (page 186). "The house doesn't dictate how we live," she says of her home. "It lets us be."

The homeowners in this chapter are not daunted by architecture that is less than perfect. On the contrary, they often love their spaces even more for the character of the perceived flaws. For antique textiles dealer Mathilde Labrouche, the peeling patina of an 18th-century farmhouse in southwest France (pages 188–189) provides the perfect backdrop for a household filled with unusual and handmade objects. On Long Island, decorator and modern art fan James Huniford removed a drywall ceiling to expose his home's Corten-steel beaming (page 204). Most people would have covered up this architectural underpinning, but Huniford saw beauty in necessity and left the beams exposed.

It takes confidence to trust your instincts and design a home that tells a story—your story. Family and friends may question your choices, but the results will feel unique and timeless. The main design lesson on these pages? When it comes to decorating, the best rules to follow are the ones that you yourself make up along the way.

"IN MY EXPERIENCE, WOMEN ARE OFTEN MORE MASCULINE AND FORWARD IN THEIR SENSE OF COLOR THAN PEOPLE THINK"

Alex Papachristidis, interior designer

ABOVE: In the living room of a London duplex designed for a divorced woman by Alex Papachristidis, the focal point is a striking 19th-century Italian male nude, which once belonged to the dancer Rudolf Nureyev. The room's furnishings include Syrie Maugham chairs, vintage sconces, and an ormolu-mounted Regency desk.

FACING PAGE: A lover of strong color, interior designer Bruno de Caumont painted the living area of his Brussels attic apartment three shades of blue, from cobalt to navy, and added bright orange accents in

the form of sconce shades and a lacquer cocktail table. The antique mirror is English and the Empire console is mahogany. The Regence chairs—also in blue and orange— were purchased at a Paris flea market.

PAGE 174: In his London apartment, photographer Simon Upton displays furniture, objects, and art culled from his global travels. In the dining and work area, Arts and Crafts chairs flank a French fabric-cutter's table. The wall is hung with his photographs as well as animal horns, a South African Zulu hat, and other artwork.

FACING PAGE: Artist and textile designer Susan Hable Smith painted the front parlor of her home in Athens, Georgia, in her favorite paint color: Benjamin Moore's Paisley Pink. The room's quirky furnishings include an antique Indonesian daybed upholstered in Moroccan wedding blankets and a cocktail table she fashioned out of a vintage shipping pallet.

BELOW: Shoe designer Brian Atwood's living room in Milan, which he decorated with help from interior designer Nate Berkus and architect Matteo Bermani, features a circa-1970 desk, vintage swivel chair, and wood-and-chrome credenza. Atwood upholstered the vintage Milo Baughman armchair in a suede he uses for his footwear and accessory designs.

RIGHT: In Estée Lauder executive John Demsey's New York townhouse, which was decorated by Bibi Monnahan, the master bedroom has bold blue walls and red accents. The rug is by Tuleh designer Bryan Bradley for Roubini.

In the great room of their home in Morocco, blogger and human rights activist Maryam Montague and her husband, architect Chris Redecke, created a seating area filled with objects and accessories culled from their travels, including pillows made from a Malian blanket and Frank Gehry Wiggle chairs adorned with vintage Indian belts.

"THIS IS MY
EXPERIMENT IN LIVING
WITH JUST ENOUGH.
IF I INTRODUCE ANYTHING
NEW, SOMETHING
HAS TO GO"

Richard McGeehan,
interior designer

LEFT: Interior designer Richard McGeehan's country house in Lake Geneva, Wisconsin, which he nicknamed Hog House, has a dining area with pine board walls and a cement floor original to the structure, a former pigpen. An antique pendant light hangs above a Paul McCobb dining table, which is surrounded by 1950s French chairs.

ABOVE: In their home in Marrakesh, Caitlin and Samuel Dowe-Sandes, owners of tile company Popham Design, furnished their daughter's bedroom with a vintage iron bed, an old map of the world, and several deer heads. The floor, which resembles a starry night, is laid with their own handmade cement tiles.

ABOVE: Steven Johanknecht, a cofounder of the California design firm Commune, created a cozy master bedroom beneath the eaves of his 1928 Tudor-style cottage in Los Angeles. The room, which is furnished with books, textiles, and taxidermy he collects, contains a George Nelson bed and a vintage zebrawood credenza.

RIGHT: The family room of fashion editor Kim Hersov's London row house is filled with artwork and textiles and one-of-a-kind furnishings, such as a carved African chair, a custom-made ottoman studded with buttons from a vintage military coat, and a 1950s light fixture from Brazil. A painting by Shezad Dawood hangs above the fireplace.

ABOVE: Interior designer Michael S. Smith turned the dining room of his New York pied-à-terre into the master bedroom. The room, which has the atmosphere of a gentleman explorer's lair, is furnished with a German-silver bed made in Jaipur, India, curtains of a Fortuny fabric, and 19th-century Dufour wallpaper panels of exotic Incan scenes.

LEFT: Picasso book plates, as well as an Eric Fischl drawing, decorate the walls of the Paris living room of rug designer Sabine de Gunzburg. The apartment, which was designed by Jacques Grange, features custom-made sofas, vintage parchment-covered chairs, and bamboo side tables, as well as a rug by de Gunzburg.

FACING PAGE: In the rural Connecticut 1950s Cape Cod home of Linda Zelenko and the late Stephen Piscuskas, owners of the custom furniture firm York Street Studio, the outdoor dining terrace is furnished with café-style wood slat chairs and a concrete-plank table of their own design.

In southwest France, vintage textiles dealer Mathilde Labrouche painted the walls of her family's 18th-century farmhouse with a homemade concoction of traditional pigments and rabbit-skin glue. The room is furnished with a custom-made sofa and a canopy bed. A religious painting and antique mercury-glass are displayed on shelving that came from a textile shop.

LEFT: Decorator Todd Alexander Romano made the most of every inch of his 350-square-foot Manhattan living room, where the exuberant scheme includes more than 15 pieces of furniture as well as Op Art on the walls and a vintage Mongolian lamb's wool rug.

FACING PAGE: Artist Kazumi Yoshida, who designs fabrics and wallpapers for Clarence House, furnished the living room of his Tribeca apartment with matching Milo Baughman sofa and armchairs, a Vladimir Kagan cocktail table, a rug of his own design, and a wall lamp by Jean Prouvé.

WHAT THE PROS KNOW: *MIX MASTERS*

CROSS TALK

A home's layout should enhance the way you like to live. The artist and textile designer Kazumi Yoshida—who delights in what he calls "making conversations"—asked his designer, Alan Tanksley, for a living room with a seating arrangement that would accommodate the small gatherings of friends he loves to host, opposite. For Yoshida, objects, too, can have their own dialogue: The room's furnishings, which range from Art Deco to 1970s modern, are happily engaged in their own stylistic conversation.

AROUND THE WORLD

In her home in Morocco, human rights activist and blogger Maryam Montague has furnished a great room with furniture and objects gathered from her travels, on pages 180–181. She unifies the disparate elements by creating a series of intimate seating areas within the large space—each anchored by a vintage Moroccan Berber rug. Accessories from around the globe, such as shawls, belts, and beads, complete the room. "I have a very fashion-y approach to design," Montague says.

IN THE MOOD

Sometimes, the spirit of a space can dictate the decor—especially when the architecture is loaded with personality. Actress Reese Witherspoon, working with interior designer Kristen Buckingham, furnished a bedroom for her son Deacon, on page 212, with a quirky mix of objects—from a collection of white antlers to a vintage Italian mirror—that complements the idiosyncratic features of the house, a former stable designed in the 1920s by the iconic California architect Wallace Neff.

TIME TRAVELER

A gutsy design scheme works best when attention has been paid to the details. Interior designer Todd Alexander Romano's 350-square-foot Manhattan living room, above, contains no fewer than 70 pieces of furniture and art. But it's the small touches—like grosgrain ribbon set into the seams of the sofa cushions—that make the room feel coherent and special. "I am fanatically thoughtful when it comes to these things," Romano says.

TOP: Photographer Nathaniel Goldberg furnished the living room of his 1820s Greek Revival house in Columbia County, New York, with an 18th-century Swedish sofa and a trio of wood cocktail tables. He found the room's wingback chair, 1940s French iron-and-wood armchair, 1930s étagère, and 1940s American floor lamp in nearby Hudson, New York.

CENTER: The living room of Doug Turshen and Rochelle Udell's Ossining, New York, home, which was designed and renovated by Dick Bories and James Shearron, contains such midcentury classics as a Bertoia bird chair and ottoman, an Eames plywood cocktail table, and a George Nelson bench.

LEFT: The late Albert Hadley and Britton Smith (together with architect Tim Greer of Roger Ferris + Partners Architects) designed this Manhattan apartment for jewelry designer Diana Quasha, whose living room has a 1960s tapestry by Marc Saint-Saëns depicting musicians and dancers.

FACING PAGE: Designers Andrea Filippone and William Welch created a dining area from a derelict barn, one of four that they transformed into their New Jersey home. The plaster-cast mantel came from a Manhattan brownstone designed by McKim, Mead & White. The dining chairs are from Provence, and the flooring was originally beams in a Civil War hospital in Gettysburg, Pennsylvania.

LEFT: The lake room in Jennifer and James Cacioppo's home in a Jacobean Revival house in Tuxedo Park, New York—which was designed by Ernest de la Torre—has a cocktail table inspired by Jean-Michel Frank along with an assortment of vintage furnishings.

ABOVE: In Garrison, New York, homeowners Bill Burback and Peter Hoffman furnished the dining room of their 1793 Federal house with a Windsor chair, a 19th-century love seat, and an 18th-century tilt-top table. The faux-wood ceramic plates are by Paul Nelson.

"BECAUSE I WORK FROM
HOME, I WANTED A COMFORTABLE AND
SOOTHING SPACE BUT ALSO AN
ENVIRONMENT THAT CONTINUALLY
INSPIRES ME"

Claiborne Swanson Frank, photographer

LEFT: The dining room of Claiborne Swanson and James Frank's Manhattan apartment, which was decorated with the help of his mother, ELLE DECOR's contributing design editor Cynthia Frank, has a 1940s Venini chandelier, an antique table, chairs found at a Paris flea market, and paintings by Ira Yeager.

FACING PAGE: In a glamorous Paris apartment designed by Kelli Wilde and Laurent Champeau, the living room features a daybed by Armand Albert Rateau, a side table by Donghia, and a 1930s cocktail table. The sconces are by Gilles & Boissier, and the gilt-wood mirror and marble fireplace are original to the 19th-century apartment.

ANATOMY OF A ROOM

Even on the cloudiest of London days, the sitting room in Allegra Hicks's Victorian townhouse in the Chelsea neighborhood glows with personality and warmth. The designer, who was born in Italy, has brought a whimsical mix of textures and patterns to her home. "It's not a house put together in order to look good," she says. "It has been put together to remind me of my life."

- **BE YOURSELF** "To me a house should be like the way you dress," Hicks says. "It should reflect your personality." Her mantel, for instance, holds a collection of art and objects she holds dear. And just as Hicks's personal style is a mix of classic and modern, her sitting room effortlessly combines antiques like a Louis XVI sofa with the contemporary S chair designed by her friend Tom Dixon.

- **WARM IT UP** The light in London, Hicks says, "can be very white and cold." She uses rich, evocative colors such as the sitting room's ocher and aqua as a counterbalance. The yellow walls make the room feel sunny even on rainy days. To give them even more depth, Hicks had the walls varnished in a subtle patchwork texture, which provides a soft contrast with the highly patterned rug.

- **ART OF LIVING** For Hicks, no room is complete without art. The sitting room has 1930s watercolors by Francesco Clemente over the sofa, but Hicks is just as likely to display artwork by friends or drawings by her daughters.

- **NATURAL WORLD** Personal spaces often incorporate elements inspired by the homeowner's passions. Hicks, an ardent gardener and nature lover, noticed an insect with unusual wings in her garden. She made a sketch of the strange bug and transformed the design into the pattern of the room's striking turquoise rug.

ABOVE: Decorator Larry Laslo designed the sofas and cocktail table in his living room in Palm Beach, Florida. The ottoman is by Christopher Guy, the 1930s marble-top side table is by Gilbert Poillerat, and the 1920s mirror on the pedestal is by Armand Albert Rateau.

RIGHT: A guest cottage on Michel Botbol and Arthur Krystofiak's Long Island, New York, country estate contains a twig bed dressed in vintage Hudson's Bay Co. blankets. A beehive was fashioned into a ceiling light fixture, and the floor lamp is from the estate of Geoffrey Beene.

In textile designer John Robshaw's living room on New York's Lower East Side, which was designed in collaboration with decorator Sara Bengur, deep red walls create a striking backdrop for his collection of objects from around the world, including Turkish calligraphy mirrors and a wood cow sculpture. The John Derian sofa is upholstered in one of Robshaw's linen prints and topped with his pillows. The bone-inlay side tables hold mango-wood lamps.

FACING PAGE: A hoop sculpture by artist Jennifer Andrews adorns a wall in the den of decorator James Huniford's Hamptons beach house. He designed the room's wing chair and sofa, and the side tables are vintage.

TOP: In the guest room of Malibu real estate broker Chris Cortazzo's house, designer Martyn Lawrence Bullard covered the walls in a patterned linen of his own design. He also created the four-poster bed. The room's photographs are of African children.

RIGHT: Fabric designer Allegra Hicks's dining room in London has a 1940s dining table and chairs and a Venini mirror from the 1950s. She designed the room's silk wall covering, curtains, and rug.

> "I WANTED
> THE PLACE TO HAVE AN
> EASY GLAMOUR
> ABOUT IT, MORE PARIS
> IN THE 1970s
> THAN THE 1940s"
>
> *Jackie Astier, stylist*

ABOVE: In the master bedroom of public relations executive Roberto Begnini's apartment in Rome, which is located within a 17th-century palazzo, a silk-paneled screen from the late 1800s shields the custom-made four-poster bed from the light that streams into the space through the large window. The toile wallpaper is by Colefax and Fowler.

RIGHT: Stylist and editor Jackie Astier furnished the library of her Manhattan apartment with a Dunbar sofa and a striking 1970s brass Mastercraft cocktail table. A Damien Hirst etching hangs on the wall, which is covered in faux-bois wallpaper.

FACING PAGE: Decorator Steven Volpe's San Francisco loft has a living area filled with art and collectible furniture, including a vintage Mongolia lambskin chair by Franco Albini, and a painting by Jef Verheyen. The linen velvet sofa was designed by Volpe.

RIGHT: Skylights flood photographer Simon Upton's London bedroom with natural light. The room is furnished with a canopied four-poster bed along with a globe-trotting assortment of decorative accessories and art, including a South African zebra skin, decorative kudu horns, and a drawing by Robbie Duff-Scott.

WHAT THE PROS KNOW: *ARTFUL TOUCHES*

COLOR CUE

A singular artwork can serve as a departure point for a room's design. Jewelry designer Diana Quasha described her home's neutral palette as "ice princess"—that is, until she imported a series of vibrant tapestries featuring musicians by Marc Saint-Saëns. The green-and-blue section of the tapestry that hangs in the living area (page 192) brings the room to life and is echoed in the palette of jewel-tone cushions and cerulean-blue fabric on the white lacquered chairs.

OBJECT LESSON

Unusual objects and artifacts add verve to a space and serve as conversation starters. In his London loft, above, photographer Simon Upton furnishes his living room with such objects from his travels as a West African chieftain's bed, suzani textiles, Kenyan spears, and Chinese feng shui boards.

LIMITED EDITION

Personal decorating involves becoming your own curator. The San Francisco decorator Steven Volpe, for instance, chooses art, furniture, and objects that "mesh art and decor"—from a vintage John Dickinson console in tin and brass shaped to look like drapery, to conceptual art and collectible contemporary furniture by designers like Ron Arad. "I'd rather have a few things with integrity than a roomful of junk," says Volpe, whose loft is shown at left.

HEIRLOOM CHIC

European homes often have an innate sense of character that comes from a layering of objects over time. Get the look by mixing family heirlooms into your spaces. In Doug Turshen's Georgian-style home in Ossining, New York (page 192), a rococo wall clock that belonged to his grandmother has a place of honor in an otherwise minimalist living room.

In the Madrid apartment of Carolina Herrera Baez and Miguel Baez, the fashion designer—the daughter of Carolina Herrera—is constantly redecorating the living room. "That room has changed nine thousand times," she says. Here, it is furnished with a campaign bed fitted with a mattress and bolsters in a Pierre Frey fabric, an 18th-century Venetian chair, and a 19th-century bergère.

LEFT: Decorator Kristin Buckingham helped her friend, actress Reese Witherspoon, to furnish her ranch in Ojai, California. Witherspoon's son Deacon's room has a built-in bed that is original to the house, which was designed by Wallace Neff in 1923 as stables.

BELOW: A master of intriguing juxtapositions, decorator Alex Papachristidis paired a vintage cherry sideboard in a client's London living room with a graphic photograph by Paola Pivi. A Baguès cocktail table fitted with a new lacquered top holds a Karl Springer box.

FACING PAGE: In decorator Lorenzo Castillo's apartment in a 17th-century former convent in Madrid, the master bedroom includes a tapestry by Rubens, a 17th-century octagonal mirror, and a 19th-century neo-Gothic dressing table. The wallpaper was designed by Castillo.

"A HOME SHOULD BE A DISTILLATION
OF YOUR INTERESTS, OF WHO YOU REALLY ARE.
IF YOU'RE HAPPY WITH YOUR
LIFE, YOUR SPACE WILL REFLECT THAT"

Rafael de Cárdenas, interior designer

FACING PAGE: Andrew Corrie and Harriet Maxwell Macdonald, owners of the Ochre and Canvas home shops, furnished the living area of their Manhattan loft with a tufted sofa rescued from a grandmother's barn in Scotland. The hand-carved mantel was inspired by one in the library of Sir John Soane's house in London, the tin ceiling is original, and the floor is whitewashed pine.

ABOVE: Exhuberant vintage wallpaper contrasts with an equally vivid patterned rug by Madeline Weinrib in the New York dining room of Stila makeup founder Jeanine Lobell and actor Anthony Edwards. The room, which was designed by Rafael de Cárdenas, features a Gustavian-style table, cabinet, and mirror from Sweden.

In his home in a renovated warehouse on an island near Santorini, hotelier Costis Psychas created a whitewashed living room furnished with low tables that were originally used for making flatbread. The room's floors were handmade from a mix of white cement and sand. The wool pillows and cotton rugs were handwoven in Greece.

ANATOMY OF A ROOM

The dining area in decorator Philip Gorrivan's family apartment in Manhattan has a dose of Parisian élan that feels sophisticated but doesn't sacrifice kid-friendly comfort. Gorrivan's design choices are unpredictable, resulting in a unique and eye-catching space that epitomizes today's ideal mix of contemporary and classic.

- **ON THE CORNER** With limited space, Gorrivan and his wife, Lisa, need the rooms in their apartment to multitask for their family. He carved out a dining area in a corner of the living room. The banquette helps to anchor the space and create the feeling of a room within a room.

- **TIMES TWO** Rather than furnish the space with the customary long dining table, Gorrivan designed a pair of square limed-oak tables in the style of Jean-Michel Frank. Having two tables instead of one allows for maximum flexibility. "I designed this apartment for the way we live," he says. "The kids do their homework on the dining room tables." And when he hosts larger dinner parties, Gorrivan connects the tables with an adjoining leaf, which allows even more seating when needed.

- **WALL GALLERY** The designer also set the dining space apart by filling the walls gallery-style with European Old Master drawings, which he has collected for more than twenty years. The wide-ranging collection gets a unified look from a variety of gold frames, whose color is echoed in the hue of the tables.

- **BY CONTRAST** The banquette's bold striped upholstery, along with the graphic design of the carpet, could have given the space a contemporary vibe. But the antique drawings and Louis XVI–style chairs in taupe leather and embroidery establish an elegant tone.

219

SOURCEBOOK

ACCESSORIES
Asprey
asprey.com

Cartier
cartier.com

Creel and Gow
creelandgow.com

Dransfield & Ross
dransfieldandross.biz

Hermès
hermes.com

Kate Spade
katespade.com

Smythson
smythson.com

Tiffany & Co.
tiffany.com

William-Wayne & Co.
william-wayne.com

ANTIQUES
1stdibs
1stdibs.com

Balsamo Antiques
balsamoantiques.com

Bernd Goeckler
Antiques
bgoecklerantiques.com

Blackman Cruz
blackmancruz.com

De Vera
deveraobjects.com

Galerie Van den Akker
galerievandenakker.com

JF Chen
jfchen.com

John Rosselli
Antiques
johnrosselliantiques.com

John Salibello
johnsalibello.com

Liz O'Brien
lizobrien.com

Maison Gerard
maisongerard.com

Todd Merrill Studio
toddmerrillstudio.com

Wyeth
wyethhome.com

BED/BATH LINENS
Ann Gish
anngish.com

The Company Store
thecompanystore.com

Deborah Sharpe
Linens
deborahsharpelinens.com

D. Porthault
dporthault.fr

Frette
frette.com

Garnet Hill
garnethill.com

Lacoste
lacoste.com

Leontine Linens
leontinelinens.com

Libeco
libeco.com

Matouk
matouk.com

Pratesi
pratesi.com

Scandia Home
scandiahome.com

Sferra
sferra.com

Yves Delorme
yvesdelorme.com

EMPORIUM
ABC Carpet & Home
abchome.com

Aero
aerostudios.com

Ankasa
ankasa.com

Apartment 48
apartment48.com

Arhaus
arhaus.com

ArmaniCasa
armanicasa.com

Arteriors Home
Arteriorshome.com

Avenue Road
avenue-road.com

Barneys New York
barneys.com

Bergdorf Goodman
bergdorfgoodman.com

Bottega Veneta
bottegaveneta.com

Calvin Klein Home
calvinklein.com

Canvas
canvashomestore.com

Casamidy
casamidy.com

Crate and Barrel
crateandbarrel.com

Design Within Reach
dwr.com

Dwell Studio
dwellstudio.com

Flair
flairhomecollection.com

Hollyhock
hollyhockinc.com

Holly Hunt
hollyhunt.com

Hollywood at Home
hollywoodathome.com

Horchow
horchow.com

Intérieurs
interieurs.com

Jayson Home
jaysonhome.com

Jean de Merry
jeandemerry.com

John Derian
johnderian.com

John Robshaw
Textiles
johnrobshaw.com

Jonathan Adler
jonathanadler.com

Lars Bolander
larsbolander.com

Matter
mattermatters.com

Mecox Gardens
mecox.com

Neiman Marcus
neimanmarcus.com

Ochre
ochre.net

Oly
olystudio.com

Property
propertyfurniture.com

Ralph Lauren Home
ralphlaurenhome.com

Ralph Pucci
ralphpucci.net

Restoration Hardware
rh.com

Room & Board
roomandboard.com

Safavieh
safavieh.com

Soane
soane.co.uk

Suite New York
suiteny.com

Terrain
shopterrain.com

The Future Perfect
thefutureperfect.com

Todd Alexander Romano
toddromanohome.com

Treillage
treillageny.com

Williams-Sonoma Home
wshome.com

FLOOR COVERINGS
Beauvais Carpets
beauvaiscarpets.com

Carini Lang
carinilang.com

Christopher Farr
christopherfarr.com

Dash & Albert
dashandalbert.com

Elson & Co.
elsoncompany.com

FJ Hakimian
fjhakimian.com

Fort Street Studio
fortstreetstudio.com

Madeline Weinrib
madelineweinrib.com

Mansour Modern
mansourmodern.com

Odegard
odegardinc.com

The Rug Company
therugcompany.com

Stark
starkcarpet.com

Tai Ping
taipingcarpets.com

Tufenkian
tufenkian.com

Warp & Weft
warpandweft.com

FURNITURE
Andrianna Shamaris
andriannashamarisinc.com

B&B Italia
bebitalia.it

Baker
bakerfurniture.com

Baxter
baxter.it

BDDW
bddw.com

Bernhardt
bernhardt.com

BoConcept
boconcept.com

Calligaris
calligaris.it

Carl Hansen & Son
carlhansen.com

Cassina
cassina.com

Century Furniture
centuryfurniture.com

Christian Liaigre
christian-liaigre.fr

Christopher Guy
christopherguy.com

DDC
ddcnyc.com

Ethan Allen
ethanallen.com

Fendi
fendi.com

Fritz Hansen
fritzhansen.com

George Smith
georgesmith.com

Hickory Chair
hickorychair.com

Julian Chichester
julianchichester.com

Knoll
knoll.com

Lee Industries
leeindustries.com

Ligne Roset
ligne-roset-usa.com

McGuire
mcguirefurniture.com

Minotti
minotti.com

Mitchell Gold +
Bob Williams
mgandbw.com

Molteni
molteni.it

Natuzzi
natuzzi.com

Roche Bobois
rochebobois.com

Rose Tarlow
Melrose House
rosetarlow.com

KITCHEN/BATH
Bertazzoni
bertazzoni.com

Boffi
boffi.com

Brizo
brizo.com

Bulthaup
bulthaup.com

Dornbracht
dornbracht.com

Duravit
duravit.com

GE
geappliances.com

Jenn-Air
jennair.com

Kallista
kallista.com

Kohler
kohler.com

Miele
miele.com

Samsung
samsung.com

Scavolini
scavolini.us

Siematic
siematic.us

Sub-Zero
subzero.com

Thermador
thermador.com

Viking
vikingrange.com

Waterworks
waterworks.com

Wolf
wolfappliance.com

LIGHTING
Artemide
artemide.us

Christopher Spitzmiller
christopherspitzmiller.com

Circa Lighting
circalighting.com

Flos
flos.com

Hudson Valley Lighting
hudsonvalleylighting.com

Lindsey Adelman
lindseyadelman.com

Roll & Hill
rollandhill.com

Schoolhouse Electric
schoolhouseelectric.com

Sonneman
sonneman.com

Urban Electric
urbanelectricco.com

Visual Comfort & Co.
visualcomfort.com

Ylighting
ylighting.com

PAINT
Benjamin Moore
benjaminmoore.com

Divine Color
devinecolor.com

Donald Kaufman
Color
donaldkaufmancolor.com

Farrow & Ball
farrow-ball.com

Glidden
glidden.com

Sherwin-Williams
sherwin-williams.com

Valspar Paint
valsparpaint.com

TABLETOP
Baccarat
baccarat.com

Bernardaud
bernardaud.fr

Christofle
christofle.com

Juliska
juliska.com

Kneen & Co.
kneenandco.com

Lenox
lenox.com

L'Objet
l-objet.com

Match
match1995.com

Michael Aram
michaelaram.com

Michael C. Fina
michaelcfina.com

Moser
moserusa.com

Mottahedeh
mottahedeh.com

Puiforcat
puiforcat.com

Reed & Barton
reedandbarton.com

Richard Ginori
richardginori1735usa.com

Saint-Louis
Crystal
saint-louis.com

Sur La Table
surlatable.com

Vietri
vietri.com

Waterford
waterford.com

Wedgwood
wedgwood.com

William Yeoward
Crystal
williamyeowardcrystal.com

TEXTILES/
WALLCOVERINGS
Brunschwig & Fils
brunschwig.com

Clarence House
clarencehouse.com

Cowtan & Tout
cowtan.com

Dedar
dedar.com

de Gournay
degournay.com

de Le Cuona
delecuona.com

Donghia
donghia.com

Holland & Sherry
hollandandsherry.com

Jim Thompson
jimthompson.com

Kravet
kravet.com

Lee Jofa
leejofa.com

Les Indiennes
lesindiennes.com

Osborne & Little
osborneandlittle.com

Perennials
perennialsfabrics.com

Phillip Jeffries
phillipjeffries.com

Pierre Frey
pierrefrey.com

Schumacher
fschumacher.com

Sunbrella
sunbrella.com

Zimmer + Rohde
zimmer-rohde.com

TILE/SURFACE
Ann Sacks
annsacks.com

Antolini
antolini.com

Artistic Tile
artistictile.com

Bisazza
bisazza.com

Caesarstone
caesarstoneus.com

DuPont Corian
dupont.com

Exquisite Surfaces
xsurfaces.com

Sicis
sicis.com

Silestone
silestoneusa.com

PHOTO CREDITS